TAKING GOD AT HIS WORD.

Why the Bible should be taken literally.

DAVID P. LEAK

Taking God at His Word

"For I am not ashamed of the Gospel of Christ; for it is the power of God unto salvation to everyone that believeth..." (Romans 1:16)

Chapter 1: The Bible is historically true. *"But if ye believe not his writings, how shall ye believe my words?"* (John 5:47).

    a.   The Bible has survived historical criticism.
    b.   Who wrote the Bible and when was it written?
    c.   Why are there so many mistakes in the Bible?
    d.   Has archeology provided any evidence supporting the Bible?
    e.   The historic accuracy concerning Jesus:
    f.   Did Jesus exist? Was Jesus crucified and did he die?
    g.   Did Jesus really raise from the dead?

Chapter 2: The Bible is scientifically reliable. *"If I have told you earthly things, and ye believe not, how shall ye believe, if I tell you of heavenly things."* (John 3:12).

    a.   Science originated and higher education was advanced by Bible believing Christians.
    b.   The Bible provides the most scientifically reliable explanation of the origin of the universe.
    c.   The Bible provides the most scientifically reliable explanation of the origin of life.
    d.   The Bible provides the most scientifically reliable explanation of the origin of human life.
    e.   The Bible provides the most scientifically reliable explanation of the diversity of languages.

f. The Bible's account of a global flood is scientifically reliable.

g. The Bible's description of miracles can be explained.

h. The Bible was the first to describe many scientific facts we understand today.

i. The Bible's description of God as a trinity is scientifically appropriate.

Chapter 3: The Bible is prophetically accurate. *"Show the things that are come here after, that we may know that ye are gods.* (Isaiah 41:23).

    a. The Bibles prediction of the fall of 4 ancient cities.

    b. The prophecies of Daniel that have been fulfilled.

    c. The Eastern Gate prophecy.

    d. The history of Israel fulfills Biblical prophecy.

    e. The prophecies of Jesus Birth.

    f. The prophecies of Jesus life found in Isaiah 53.

    g. The prophecies of Jesus crucifixion found in Psalm 22.

    h. A brief overview of Revelation

Chapter 4: The Bible is spiritually sound. *"Let us hear the conclusion of the whole matter: fear God, and keep his commandments; for this is the whole duty of man."* (Ecc.12:13).

    a. We are created in the image of God.

    b. We are sinful by nature.

    c. God loves sinners.

    d. Sinners must place faith in Jesus Christ

    e. Once saved we should live a life of love.

    f. Encouraging scriptures

Special thanks to my Grandaddy Paschal.

I would also strongly encourage you to check out Faith Bible Institute. Most of what is included in this book came from the things I learned from John Yates instruction in a three year in depth study of God's Word.

www.faithbibleinstitute.com/register.html

"Heaven and earth shall pass away: but my words shall not pass away."

Luke 21:33

Introduction

As a child I remember getting up early on Sunday morning and going to Sunday school. It was there I was taught incredible stories from the Bible. I learned about David and Goliath, Daniel and the Lion's den, Jonah and the big fish, Noah and the flood...every Sunday I learned another amazing story from the Bible. I was fascinated by these Bible stories and as I grew up I learned many important truth's found in the Bible. I learned about Jesus who was born of a virgin, Mary, in a stable with the animals. I learned how Jesus grew up and lived a perfect life, performing miracles, healing the sick, and teaching powerful truths of God's love. Then I learned why this loving man who lived a perfect life had to be crucified. For years I could not understand why.

I remember distinctly the moment it finally clicked for me. I was 11 years old when I realized that I was a sinner. I was living a life apart from God and I was lost. As I studied the Bible I discovered Jesus chose to be crucified so he could pay the debt of sin that I owed. It was then I fell in love with Jesus and surrendered my heart to him, I have never been the same. My faith continued to grow through High School as I was surrounded by friends who shared my faith. We all were taught that the Bible is God's Word and that we should live our lives guided by its truth. There were a few who did not share my faith but no one ever challenged my faith until I went to college.

I was sitting in one of my first college classes and the professor stated quite definitively that absolute truth does not exist. She said that anyone who claimed to have or understand absolute truth was either incredibly naive or so audacious and bigoted

i

that they would never accept any other belief. This left me a little bewildered and I began to doubt my own faith in the Bible.

Could I be so naïve as to think the Bible alone contained absolute truth? I began to study other religions and philosophies. I read the Koran, the Torah, even the Book of Mormon. I studied the philosophies of Aristotle, Socrates, and Niche... It was truly eye opening to realize how many different views are out there. I was now much more sophisticated and I relished being able to discuss different philosophies with others. I questioned how I ever believed the Bible to be absolutely true. Several years passed by and I became active in Church again, but I continued to study other religions and philosophies. The more I studied the more I began to notice how unique the Bible really was. Sure there were other religious books but none were as profound or as persuasive as the Bible. I was in a weird place spiritually. I claimed to be a Christian but I was having a hard time balancing my Christian faith with the many other philosophies I was studying.

Then one night I was watching Rick Warren, author of A Purpose driven life, being interviewed by Larry King. He was asked whether or not he ever doubted his Christian faith. His answer changed my life. He said yes, of course he had doubts but he doubted his doubts and believed his beliefs. WOW! I loved it.[1] I had gone through many years of doubt but I could not shake my belief in the Bible. I read "Mere Christianity" by C.S. Lewis And "Reason for God" by Timothy Keller then I enrolled in The Faith Bible Institute, by John Yates. This in depth study of God's Word renewed my faith and inspired me to write this book. The Bible is the absolute truth of God's Word. You can take God at His Word. So can truth be known?[2]

Introduction

Is truth relative or absolute? If absolute truth exists, how do we know if something is absolutely true? These are questions philosophers have pondered throughout human history. If you spend any time on the internet you will find endless websites with endless views on truth. In the 17th century French philosopher Rene Descartes became obsessed with the idea of absolute truth or certainty. Interestingly Descartes was a devout Roman Catholic, yet he replaced God as the starting place for knowledge with his own ability to find truth. He famously said "I think, therefore I am." His quest for truth started modern philosophy. Descartes believed in absolute truth and he spent his life trying to find the absolute truth in many areas of life such as ethics, mathematics, and even politics.

Later philosophers such as Georg Wilhelm Friedrich Hegel attempted to place everything in some order thinking that if truth is attainable it would need to be studied, and placed in separate area's in order to be easily understood and practiced. This created systems like Marxism, Nazism, Socialism, capitalism, and many other "isms". Some of these "isms" tended to oppress those who did not fit into the system. Such as the Jews in Nazi Germany. This resulted in the rise of Postmodernism which says that there is no such thing as absolute truth. Truth is something that varies depending on each person's circumstances, background, and viewpoints. Each person's truth is just as valid as anyone else's truth. No truth is objectively true or false. A person's truth is really nothing more than a person's opinion. This has led to the relativism that has become widely popular today. The question becomes is truth absolute or relative?

Introduction

Today we have the unique ability to closely investigate everyone's thoughts and beliefs which makes understanding truth more difficult. This has caused most people in the world to have a postmodern view of truth. What is post-modernism?[2]

Post-modernism says that each person dictates what is or isn't true for themselves. No one can ever claim to have the universal absolute truth. Post-modernism celebrates diversity and questions anyone who claims to know absolute truth. To the relativist no fact is true for all people at all times, this has turned truth into opinion. So what you consider to be true, I may not and it's O.K. It doesn't matter if our views of truth contradict each other, because all ideas of truth are equally valid. There is no wonder in this hyper sensitive, politically correct, and tolerant society we live in today that post-modernism has become so widely accepted.

This is one reason that those who take a literal interpretation of the Bible are viewed as being narrow minded. According to relativist, no book can be absolutely true for everyone. The problem with relativism is that it becomes self-refuting by claiming to be the only truth which everyone should accept. Relativism applies to non-relativists as well as relativist, so you see it becomes absolutely true for everyone. This means that the only people allowed to have absolute truth are those who believe absolute truth doesn't exist. So the relativist are every bit as arrogant and narrow minded as Christians.[3]

Does truth exist? Can truth be known? The funny thing is that we actually demand truth in every area of life. What if our banker claimed that no one could be certain of our account balance? What if our doctor claimed to be unsure of our health? What if no one could be certain of the time?

We also know who the president is, We know the New England Patriots won the Super Bowl last year, We know 1+1=2. In fact if you want to know the truth about nearly any subject, just Google it and you will (probably) get the truth. So truth can certainly be known. To say that truth cannot be known is self-defeating in that the statement itself claims to be a known truth.

Another aspect of post-modernism is the idea that all idea's and beliefs are equally valid. This idea sounds good but is not even possible. How can 2 opposing ideas be equally valid? If one person believes 1+1=3 and another person believes 1+1=2 then they can't both be right. The truth is that 1+1=2. That truth is absolute, no matter what anyone does or doesn't believe. What about morality? Can truth in morality be absolute? Relativists say no. So Is it morally wrong to torture innocent animals? Is it morally wrong to abuse little children? Is it morally wrong to have slaves? I am willing to say that moral absolutes do exist.

Another more common question is does truth in morality matter? Again, relativists say no. Geisler and Turek bring up some valid points in their book "I don't have enough faith to be an atheist." Did it matter that the United States Supreme Court believed that blacks were not citizens but property in the 1857 Dredd Scott case? Did it matter that the Nazi's believed the Jews were an inferior race? Does it matter that aborting a baby is considered a choice and not a life? Yes, truth in morality can be known and it matters greatly. [5]

While I believe absolute truth exist, it has become harder and harder to find. The world we live in is bombarded by different ideas, beliefs, and thoughts, making it extremely difficult to be certain about anything any longer. This has led to millions of people who get caught up in false religions, cults, and even atheism. All of this uncertainty has caused a lapse in morality in America. We are in desperate need of moral truth today. The best source of absolute truth is the Bible. The Bible is the Word of God and every word of it is true. The reason for writing this book is to illustrate how the Bible is true in every area. The Bible is historically true, prophetically accurate, scientifically reliable, spiritually sound, and the Bible can meet practical needs.

Our country is in trouble. Radical Islamic terrorist threaten our safety, the national debt is astronomical, race relations are worse now than they were 20 years ago, and now we say it's alright if a man want's to use the women's restroom! People are grasping for anything trying to make sense of it all. The problem is that no one seems to be able to find any truth in this society. We blame these problems on greedy elitist, crooked politicians, radical Islamic terrorist, the liberal media, even global warming but none of these are the real problem of our society. The real problem in our society is the lack of absolute truth.

People mistakenly believe absolute truth does not exist, so what happens is that this allows any idea or belief to be equally valid no matter if it is true or not. We desperately need absolute truth to wisely guide our decisions which will bring the peace we all desire. So where can absolute truth be found? The only source of absolute truth I have found is the Bible. This society may be the most knowledgeable, scientifically advanced, progressive society in the history of the world, but it is also the most Biblically ignorant, morally bankrupt societies the world has ever known.

Introduction

Whose fault is it?... Christians, we have been silent. We have not presented the absolute truth of God's Word to a hurting world who desperately needs it. Why? ... There are many reasons. Fear of being rejected has always been a leading reason but today it may be because of our own lack of knowledge of the Bible. Christians today do not study the Bible or pray as much as Christians in the past have done. This has led to a lack of evangelism. Which results in a dying church. My purpose for writing this book is to encourage Christians to study God's Word and to take the truth's learned from this study and share them with a lost world who desperately need the absolute truth of God's word. This leads to an important question, is The Bible absolutely true? I say it most certainly is. In fact I believe the Bible is absolutely true in every area of life.

The Bible is historically true. The Apostle John put it this way, "But if ye believe not his writings, how shall ye believe my words?" (John 5:47). The Bible has survived the most intense historical criticism only to be found the most historically accurate ancient text in the world. The more archeologist dig the more reliable the Bible becomes. In fact Christianity is the only religion that depends on its historical truth. Christianity rises and falls on Jesus Christ. Did Jesus even exist? Was he crucified and more importantly did he rise from the grave? If he did then Christianity is not simply a religion it is historical fact and everyone ever born must decide for themselves what Jesus resurrection means.

The Bible is scientifically reliable. Jesus said. "If I have told you earthly things, and ye believe not, how shall ye believe, if I tell you of heavenly things." (John 3:12). Today there is this notion that the Bible is against science and that science has made the Bible obsolete. There is nothing farther from the truth. Science was advanced by Bible believing Christians. The Bible provides the most scientifically reliable explanation of the origin of the universe, the origin of life and the diversity of languages. The Bible's account of a global flood is scientifically reliable. The Bible's description of miracles can be explained. In fact the Bible was the first to describe many scientific facts we understand today. One of these is how the Bible describes God as a trinity. As a Christian who loves science this chapter is my favorite.

The Bible is prophetically accurate. The great prophet Isaiah wrote "Show the things that are come here after, that we may know that ye are gods. (Isaiah 41:23). There are many text that are historically true but none are as prophetically accurate as the Bible. The Bible is the only religious book to contain any accurate prophecies. These prophecies are not ambiguous like Nostradamus, they are incredibly specific. The Bible predicted the fall of 4 ancient cities. The prophet Daniel made many very specific prophecies concerning Alexander the Great. Then there are the hundreds of prophecies fulfilled by Jesus. One of the most incredible prophecies concern Jerusalem's Eastern Gate. The nation of Israel itself is powerful proof of Biblical prophecy. Of course there is the book of Revelation which is full of prophecies. We will look at all of these in this book.

The Bible is spiritually sound. Solomon contemplated many philosophies and came to this conclusion...let us hear the conclusion of the whole matter: fear God, and keep his commandments; for this is the whole duty of man." (Ecc.12:13).

Introduction

In this chapter we will look at some basic spiritual truths found in the Bible. The first being that we are created in the image of God. We are sinful by nature but thankfully God loves sinners. We must be born again by placing our faith in Jesus Christ. We are saved unto good works not by good works. And finally our Salvation is eternally sound. When we understand these spiritual truths it brings purpose, peace, and joy to our lives.

The wonderful truth is the Bible is not just a history book, or prophetic book, or a book of science, or even a simple book of morals. The truths found in the Bible meet any need you may have, God speaks directly to each of us through His Word the Bible. I truly hope this book will inspire you to study God's word.

The Bible is Historically True

"But if ye believe not his writings, how shall ye believe my words?" (John 5:47)

Is the Bible in fact the Word of God, or just another religious book? One of the most obvious distinctions between the Bible and other religious books is that the Bible serves to record history as well as spiritual truths. This is unique in that it captures the history of God as He interacts with His beloved creation. The Bible gives a rather detailed account of God's chosen people, the nation of Israel. No other religious work details the history of people and places like the Bible does. This leaves the Bible open to scrutiny, and it appears that no book has been as scrutinized as the Bible. We will begin this chapter by looking at how well the Bible has withstood historical criticism.

We will answer a few common questions that have been raised concerning the Bible such as: Who wrote the Bible and when was it written? How can one explain the reported mistakes and contradictions found in the Bible? Has archeology provided any evidence to support the Bible? Finally we will answer a few important questions about Jesus. Did Jesus really exist? Was Jesus crucified? Did Jesus actually rise from the dead? Today's internet contains many sites that question the reliability of the Bible. When you couple this with the low number of people who have actually read the Bible in its entirety, you have a Bible which may seem outdated, unimportant, or unreliable. This can cause even the most faithful Christian to doubt whether the Bible is literally God's Word or if it is merely a collection of

1

fables intended to act as a moral compass. I truly believe as you inspect these questions you will find the Bible to be amazingly trustworthy.

The Bible has survived historical criticism: The Bible has been the most attacked, most censured and banned book in all of history. It was actually attacked even before it was compiled. In AD 303 Emperor Diocletian attempted to have all Christian records and letters destroyed. Anyone claiming to be a Christian or in possession of Christian literature was put to death. After years of tyrannizing Christians and burning all Christian literature, Diocletian erected a column of victory with the inscription, "***Extinct is the name Christian.***" It would seem as though Christianity had ended before the first Bible was ever compiled.

Fortunately, only 20 years after Diocletian declared Christianity extinct, his successor Constantine declared Rome a Christian nation and offered a hefty reward to anyone who could produce Christian literature. In less than three weeks Constantine collected enough literature to compile dozens of Bibles.

The attack on the Bible continued into the middle ages when a number of Roman Catholic Popes opposed any translation or distribution of the Bible. In AD 1199 Pope Innocent III ordered the burning of all Bibles, and in AD 1529 William Tyndale was deported from England for publishing the Bible. Fortunately, Tyndale was undeterred as he moved to Germany where he subsequently printed thousands of Bibles. Ironically, Tyndale was able to continue printing Bibles in large part due to the fact that the Roman Catholic Church had purchased and destroyed all copies of his Bibles they could locate, which in turn helped fund Tyndale's work.

The Bible is Historically True.

In AD 1555 Mary Queen of England, nicknamed "Bloody Mary" declared it illegal to be a Protestant and burned many Christians at the stake along with copies of the Bible that could be found. Five years after her untimely death, her successor, Queen Elizabeth I, published 130 editions of the Bible.[1]

In 1750, French writer Voltaire stated, *"Another century and there will be not a Bible on Earth!"* After Voltaire's death in 1778 his house was purchased, along with his printing press, by the Geneva Bible Society. They printed copies of the Bible on Voltaire's printing press and used his house as a depot for Bibles which were eventually distributed worldwide. The Bible not only survived censorship and attack, but has become the world's best-selling book of all time.[1]

Who wrote the Bible and when was it written? Questions abound regarding the origin of the Bible. Why is there no original text? Who wrote the Bible and when was it written? How can we trust the Bible? Although these questions were once difficult to answer, the last century has provided much more evidence that supports the Bible's reliability. The problem seems to be a general lack of interest in discovering the truth about the Bible. As to the lack of any original text, it is true that there is no portion of the Bible that can be found in its original form. This certainly would seem to be a problem. If the Bible is truly God's word, why did God not provide us with an original text?

While no one can answer this question with any certainty, take a minute to think about it. What would happen if we had an original? Would it prove that the Bible is God's word? Even if God did give us an original text, imagine the problems it could cause. An original work could be lost or stolen, it could be changed, or anyone who possessed it might use it to control others. In God's wisdom He did not preserve an original text, but what He did is nothing short of miraculous.

God inspired thirty-eight men to write sixty-six books, written in three different languages on three continents that took more than two thousand years to write and compile. Imagine the Bible as a book with sixty-six different chapters written by thirty-eight authors. The first author wrote the first five chapters before his death. Over the next thousand years, thirty different authors from vastly different backgrounds living in many different countries used their own language to add to this amazing book.

During the next four hundred years no one adds anything to the Bible. Finally, another eight authors added the last twenty-seven chapters. How could such a book even exist? How is it possible that all of them tell the same story of God's great love for the world? When you think about it, sixty-six books with thirty-eight authors writing over a period of two thousand years is remarkable. The way God chose to give us his Word makes it more reliable, not less so.

Lee Strobel, author of *The Case for the Real Jesus* interviewed Daniel B. Wallace, a professor of New Testament Studies at Dallas Theological Seminary and one of the world's most respected textual critics. Wallace spoke about the quality and quantity of the New Testament documents. Wallace claims there are more witnesses to the New Testament than any other ancient Greek or Latin literature.

There are between twenty-five and thirty thousand handwritten copies of the New Testament, fifty-seven hundred in Greek, more than ten thousand in Latin, and between ten and fifteen thousand copies of other languages including Syriac, Coptic, and Armenian. Wallace goes onto say, *"We have between ten and fifteen papyri from the 2nd Century; that's remarkable! We have for example, P66, which is from mid to late second century and has almost the entirety of John's gospel. Also, P16 which dates to about AD 200 has seven of Paul's letters and Hebrews in it. The papyri P45 is early too and it has large portions of the four Gospels. That equals about half the New Testament."* [2]

These manuscripts are ninety-eight percent identical to one another. The quantity and quality of these manuscripts is unrivalled in Roman-Greco civilization. Compare this to the next closest book, The Iliad which had but 643 manuscripts. This makes the Bible impossible to tamper with or lose, and unlikely to be worshipped. There is little doubt that with thousands of manuscripts of the sixty-six books of the Bible it remains trustworthy without a single original text. [3]

One remarkable fact concerning the reliability of the New Testament is that even if Diocletian had succeeded in destroying all copies of the Bible, we could still reconstruct nearly all of the New Testament. How, you may ask? This is because the early leaders of the Church from the second and third centuries quoted the New Testament more than thirty-six thousand times. All but eleven verses of the New Testament were quoted by men like Justin Martyr, Irenaeus, Clement of Alexandria, Origen, Tertullian, and others. In view of the overwhelming quantity and quality of manuscripts and these quotations, it is possible that not having an original may preserve God's Word better than actually having one. [3]

Geisler and Turek quote Ancient manuscript authority Frederic Kenyon in their book, *I Don't Have Enough Faith to be an Atheist.* Kenyon says, *"It cannot be too strongly asserted that in substance the text of the Bible is certain: Especially is this the case with the New Testament, of early translations from it, and of quotations from it in the oldest writers of the church, is so large that it is practically certain that the true reading of every doubtful passage is preserved in some one or other of these ancient authorities. This can be said of no other ancient book in the world."* [4]

For hundreds of years the Bible was simply accepted to be God's word written by righteous men like Moses, David, Daniel, Peter, and Paul. However, in 1682 French priest Richard Simon wrote *A Critical History of the Old Testament.* In this book he questioned whether Moses wrote the Pentenauch, whether King David existed, and whether Biblical cities such as Ur, Sodom, and Gomorrah ever existed. Simon and his theories were largely ignored until the eighteenth century when men like Friedrich Schleiermacher, a liberal German theologian and Ludwig Feurbach, a German philosopher publicly challenged the historic accuracy of the Bible and Christianity as a whole.

A growing liberal scholarly attack on the Bible's historical accuracy began. By the nineteenth century liberal colleges throughout Europe and to a lesser degree in America, taught that the Bible was not historically accurate. These biblical scholars doubted that any of the men credited with writing the books of the Bible actually wrote them. They assumed the books of the Bible were written much later than the Bible claims. However, discoveries in the past century support the Bible's claims.

The Bible is Historically True.

In March of 1947 a young shepherd boy discovered some clay pots in a cave near the Dead Sea. Once again God guided a shepherd boy to make one of the greatest archeological discoveries in history. For the next nine years, the area seven and a half miles south of Jericho and one and a half miles west of the Dead Sea was excavated.

There archeologists found more than forty thousand manuscripts primarily as fragmented of jars of clay dating two thousand years old. These manuscripts were collected, dated and studied intensively; from the thousands of manuscripts located, the entire Old Testament was compiled. Amazingly, when the texts from the two thousand year old manuscripts were examined, they were found to be ninety-seven percent identical to the Old Testament in the King James Version of today's Bible.

There remains little or no question as to the accuracy of the Old Testament. The crown jewel of the manuscripts was a twenty-four foot scroll containing all sixty-six chapters of Isaiah dating back to 100 BC. No greater book in the Old Testament points to Jesus Christ as Savior as does the book of Isaiah. It is nothing less than God's provision that preserved the entire book of Isaiah dating to a hundred years prior to Jesus' birth.

Many liberal scholars do not believe that Moses actually wrote the first 5 books of the Bible, known as the Pentateuch. Although they believe the Pentateuch was written much later, recent discoveries make the possibility that Moses did author the Pentateuch more likely. In June 1986, archeologists in Jerusalem discovered 2 silver amulets which were inscribed with portions of Numbers 6:24-26; "The *Lord bless thee, and keep thee. The Lord make his face shine upon thee, and be gracious unto thee. The Lord lift up his countenance upon thee, and give thee peace."* These amulets date to 586 BC, meaning that the Pentateuch was written much earlier than 400 BC, the date previously accepted as its origin. This discovery makes it more likely that the Pentateuch was written much earlier and there is no evidence to disprove Moses as its author.

In 1906 archeologist Flinders Petrie discovered inscriptions in a small cave in Sinai's central plains which were later identified as a very early form of the Semitic alphabet. These writings, which predate Moses' birth, may be some of the earliest forms of writing ever discovered. We know that writing certainly existed in Moses' day; as one who had access to the finest education in the world at the time, Moses would have known how to write. When you add the fact that Moses and the Israelites spent forty years wandering through the wilderness, Moses certainly had time to write the Pentateuch. It is certainly reasonable to accept the Bible's assertion that Moses was the author of the Pentateuch.[5]

The four Gospels of the New Testament have received the harshest criticism regarding who actually authored them and when they were written. Biblical scholars featured on History Channel programming often claim that there is little or no proof that Matthew, Mark, Luke, or John actually wrote the Gospels bearing their names. In fact they claim that the four gospels were not written until well after the second century. These scholars often refer to the fact that the oldest complete New Testament manuscript is the Codex Vaticanus, dating to AD 325. This is 300 years after Jesus lived.

Why is there no earlier manuscript? Recall that in AD 303 Roman Emperor Diocletian ordered the destruction of all

Christian churches, the burning of all Christian manuscripts, and the execution of anyone professing Jesus Christ. It would have been logistically impossible for Christian leaders to collect and compile the New Testament until Constantine gave the Edict of Milan in AD 313 making it legal to be a Christian.

It would not be until AD 393 at the Council of Hippo that the New Testament would be officially compiled. This is not to say it had not been written: the four Gospels were unquestioned as authentic and used in worship from the first century. There were also a number of heretical gospels written and used in worship under the assumption that they were equally inspired. This led the church to compile and canonize what is known today as the New Testament. The Council of Hippo did not arbitrarily choose the twenty-seven books of the New Testament. The writings were subject to various tests to determine their authority as God's word: Who authored the book? Was the book used in churches for instruction and worship? Does the book contradict other inspired books? In actuality, the majority of the twenty-seven books were already accepted and widely used in churches long before the council met. It was the growing number of heretical gospels being introduced in many churches that led to a need to compile a canonized New Testament.[6]

We are now quite certain that the Gospels were written much earlier than Biblical critics might believe. The John Ryland P52 fragment is the earliest known New Testament manuscript. It was recovered in Egypt and is dated to AD 117-138. It contains portions of John 18:31-38.

Another convincing proof as to the early writing of the Gospels can be found in the text itself. The Gospels were written to record the life, death, and burial of Jesus from four separate accounts, yet none mention the destruction of the Temple in Jerusalem in AD 70. This is remarkable. Imagine four present day historians living in New York City who write books without mentioning the destruction of the twin towers. You would assume that they must have written their books before September 11, 2001.

In the same way it must be assumed that all four Gospels were written before AD 70 or at least one would have mentioned the temple's destruction as Jesus predicted. When you also consider details in the Gospel, it seems reasonable to believe that the books Matthew, Mark, Luke, and John were written by followers of Jesus, Matthew, Mark, Luke, and John.

Geisler and Turek point out that the book of Acts had to be written before AD 62. They come to this conclusion because the book of Acts records the deaths of Stephen and John's brother James, but does not mention the death of James, the brother of Jesus, or the Apostle Paul. We know from Clement of Rome that Nero had the Apostle Paul put to death. We also know Nero died in AD 68.

Josephus records the death of Jesus' brother James being killed in 62 AD. We know the Gospel of Luke was written before Acts because Acts begins with this *"In my former book Theophilus, I wrote about all that Jesus began to do and to teach."* The former book Luke references is most likely his Gospel. Add to this the way Paul quotes from (Luke 10:7) and calls it scripture. (1 Timothy 5:18). This means that the Gospel of Luke must have been written before AD 60, as it must have been in circulation for at least 2 years in order to be considered scripture by AD 62.[8]

The Bible is Historically True.

The Bible is not an authorized collection of books as many claim. It actually is a collection of authorized books. Ezra is credited as the person who first began to compile scripture, and he no doubt assembled much of the Old Testament. Josephus claimed that the Old Testament was written, collected, and accepted as God's word as early as 400 BC, but was not considered canonized until AD 90. At that time, an official council of Jewish leaders ratified the Old Testament Canon at Jamnia near Joppa, Israel. The 27 New Testament books were officially canonized at the Council of Hippo in AD 393. However, twenty-three of the New Testament books had been referenced by Polycarp and Iranaeus as early as AD 170.

The oldest complete version of the Hebrew Bible is the Septuagint, dating from the 3rd century BC. The Septuagint is the Bible from which Jesus and the New Testament writers quoted. The Septuagint had no chapters or verses. These indicators were not assimilated into the Bible until the 13th century in England. The Codex Vaticanus is one of the oldest New Testament Bibles, less than 250 years after the New Testament were written. Some claim the Codex Vaticanus was among the 50 Bibles that Emperor Constantine produced after the Council of Nicea.[9]

Why are there so many mistakes in the Bible? Biblical critics claim the Bible is full of mistakes. How can we trust the Bible if it is full of mistakes and contradictions? New Testament critics cite that there are over 200,000 errors in New Testament manuscripts. This certainly seems like a serious problem for a book claiming to be God's Word. When you examine the 200,000 errors more closely it becomes quite evident that the Bible is amazingly consistent. Of the 200,000 cited errors found in New Testament manuscripts, ninety-eight percent are misspelled words. This may sound like a lot of misspelled words, but considering there are 5,700 manuscripts and each manuscript includes about 130,000 words, which includes over 741 million words. This means that only 1 of 3,700 words are misspelled. This is well before spell check—not a bad average for its time.[8]

This leaves about 4,000 variants that are more than misspelled words. The majority of these variants are due to differing word order, as *"Paul the Apostle"* in some manuscripts reads *"the Apostle Paul"* in others. Again these are technical variants that in no way change the meaning at all.

The most troubling variants found in the New Testament are those scribes intentionally changed. Critics love to point these variants out and talk about how outrageous it is that someone would intentionally change God's Word. How can anyone trust the Bible as God's word if scribes have deliberately changed the text? While this certainly sounds scandalous, it is in fact quite harmless.

The truth is that scribes have indeed purposefully changed God's Word. There are stretches of scripture that speak of Jesus but use the term *"He"*. For instance in Mark 12:43, *"And He called unto him his disciples"*, the scribe changed the word "He" to "Jesus". Now Mark 12:43 reads, *"Jesus called unto him his disciples."* This is done 89 times in scripture, and absolutely the doctrine or meaning is unchanged.

Of the over 200,000 variants cited by Biblical critics only two truly effect the meaning. These are found in Romans 5:1, where some texts read, *"**We** have peace with God through our Lord Jesus Christ"*. Other texts read, *"**Let us** have peace with God through our Lord Jesus Christ."* Similarly, 1 John 1:4 says, *"These* *things write us unto you that **your** joy may be full."* In some texts it reads, *"These things write us unto you that **our** joy may be full."* While it is technically true that these variants change the meaning of the verses, it is in no way as troubling as critics would lead you to believe. The Bible can certainly be trusted, especially when you consider that in light of all the criticism it has faced, these are the most troubling variants anyone has ever found.[9]

Aside from variants, there are other contradictions in the Bible often given attention by Biblical critics. When faced with assumed contradictions or mistakes in the Bible, I would heed the words of St. Augustine who said, *"If we are perplexed by any apparent contradiction in scripture, it is not allowable to say, the author of this book is mistaken."* It is far more likely that any perceived contradiction or mistake is from the reader and not the author of the Bible.[10]

There are six mistakes Biblical critics often make: 1.) Taking scripture out of context, 2.) Presuming God approves all that the Bible records, 3.) Assuming divergent accounts are false, 4.) Understanding when the Bible is symbolic, 5.) Basing entire doctrines on one verse, and 6.) Assuming that the unexplained is unexplainable. Inconsistencies occur when readers do not take the time to determine all the facts. Any apparent contradictions can usually be resolved when one takes time to understand the scripture.[11]

Mistake 1: Taking scripture out of context. This is the most common mistake made among even the most well intentioned students of the Bible, myself certainly included. The problem is that people can make the Bible say whatever they want simply by taking it out of context.

Here is a basic example: The Bible does contain the phrase, *"There is no God."* *This is from* Psalm 14:1 fully read as, *"The fool in his heart says, there is no God."* The meaning is clear in its context.

Mistake 2: Presuming God approves of all that the Bible records. This mistake is often made by the lost world who cannot understand how a loving God could approve of things such as slavery, chauvinism, and war. The fact is God does not approve of any of these things, but He certainly allowed them and the Bible recorded them because all were all a part of everyday life. Two of the most abused books of the Bible regarding this are Job and Ecclesiastes. Both were written from the writer's point of view, not God's.

Job 10:18-19 reads, *"Wherefore then hast thou brought me forth out of the womb? Oh that I had given up the ghost, and no eye had seen me! I should have as though I had not been; I should have been carried from my womb to the grave."* These are the words of Job during his great suffering and not an attitude approved or condoned by God. God had a purpose for Job and He has a purpose for each of us as well.

Mistake 3: Assuming divergent accounts are false. This approach is used by many of the Bible's most ardent critics, those who search the scriptures for divergent accounts in an attempt to undermine the reliability of the Bible. The most famous example is the death of Judas Iscariot. Matthew says that Judas hanged himself. (Matt 27:5) *"And he cast down the pieces of silver in the temple, and departed, and went and hanged himself."* Luke states that Judas jumped off a cliff.

(Acts 1:18) *"Now this man purchased a field with the reward of iniquity; and falling headlong, he burst asunder in the midst, and all his bowels gushed out."* This seems like a contradiction but it does not have to be.

Perhaps Judas hung himself on a tree on the side of a cliff, and at some point the branch broke and Judas' body fell off the cliff. This actually helps explain Judas' body bursting on contact, which probably would not happen simply by jumping off a cliff. If the body had been hanging in the sun, it is easy to picture his body bursting asunder as the scripture claims. As a matter of fact there are trees at the top of a cliff above Aceldama, the proclaimed Field of Blood outside Jerusalem.

Mistake 4: Understanding when scripture is symbolic and when it is literal. I believe with all my heart that the Bible is to be taken literally, and this is a major reason for writing this book. However there are certainly small portions of the Bible that are obviously symbolic. The best way to determine if a passage is literal or symbolic is to look in scripture to find the answer.

The Books of Revelation and Daniel are filled with symbolism. These symbols are usually explained later in scripture. An example is found in Rev.12:3. *"And behold a great red dragon, having 7 heads and 10 horns, and 7 crowns upon his head"*. Is this red dragon literal? If not, what does the red dragon symbolize? If you read further you discover the answer. (Rev 12:9) *"And the great dragon was cast out, that old serpent called the devil."* It is clear that the Bible uses the dragon to symbolize the devil in this instance.

Mistake 5: Basing entire doctrines on one verse. There are many denominations that base their entire doctrine on one verse to the exclusion of the remainder of scripture. I am a believer in interpreting scripture with scripture. If one verse seems to contradict the rest of scripture, one must carefully use scripture to clarify your position.

One such denomination uses Mark 16:18. *"They shall take up serpents; and if they drink any deadly thing, it shall not hurt them."* They base their entire doctrine on handling snakes and drinking poison. When you compare this one verse with the entirety of scripture it simply does not fit. While I do not doubt God protects His children from harm, I do not believe we should tempt Him by purposefully performing dangerous acts to prove our faith.

Of course there are many other verses that groups use to build their entire doctrine. There are verses that seem to indicate God's providence while other verses appear to teach free will. Some verses speak of God's great love while others speak of God's holy judgment. Some verses speak of works and others speak of grace. The Bible may seem to be full of contradictions, but when you examine the Bible as a whole and consider all verses you begin to see the larger picture. I do not claim to understand all of these, but believe it is important to place greater value on the Bible's clear teachings rather than argue over more difficult passages.

If we can agree on clear passages such as John 3:16, we become brothers and sisters in Christ and not enemies. It is important to discuss differences of opinion, but these differences should not cause Christians to turn attention from many clear teachings in God's Word. If Christians would spend more time obeying what the Bible clearly teaches, such as loving God and others, and stop arguing over differences, we would begin to witness lives being changed to have a great impact for the Kingdom of God.[14]

Mistake 6: Assuming the unexplained is unexplainable. Many Biblical truths have not been discovered by the world and may seem unexplainable, but this does not mean they will never be explained. Many laws for the priests in Leviticus, including dietary and sanitary laws were undiscovered by science 300 years ago. Today they are accepted as common knowledge based in science. These laws included such practices as washing hands to fight disease and infection and eating clean animals rather than unclean animals to maintain health.

There are also many miracles in the Bible that are dismissed by the highly educated critic. The fact that someone cannot find enough evidence to believe in an act, it does not mean it did not happen. Miracles are uncommon but not impossible. If miracles were common they would no longer be miracles at all. The story of Jonah is often dismissed as fable, yet Jesus accepted the story of Jonah as historical fact. (Matt 12:40-41) *"For as Jonas was three nights in the whale's belly so shall the Son of man be three days and three nights in the heart of the Earth. The men of Nineveh shall rise in judgment with this generation, and shall condemn it: because they repented at the preaching of Jonas; and behold, a greater than Jonas is here."*

Jesus believed that Jonah was literally swallowed by a great fish and brought to life three days later. If you have watched the television show River Monsters, you know there are enormous fish in the Mediterranean Sea that are large enough to swallow a man whole. The bigger miracle is that Jonah was cast back to the shore alive. Did he survive in the belly of the fish or did he die? I believe Jesus understood that Jonah had died in the fish's belly only to rise from the dead three days later, predicting what He would also do. The Bible is full of amazing miracles that many feel are symbolic moral lessons, but it seems far more reasonable to take God at His word and understand the miracles of the Bible as literal historical events. [14]

Has archeology provided any evidence supporting the Bible?
The historical accuracy of the Bible has been questioned from the time of its first printing. These questions spurred many archeologists to attempt to discover exactly how accurate the Bible is. The idea of locating Biblical sites began as early as the 4th century when Constantine's mother, Empress Helena identified the location of the nativity, Calvary, Jesus' empty tomb, and dozens of other sites. American clergyman Edward Robinson travelled to Jerusalem in 1837 and used his knowledge of Hebrew and the Bible to map out over 200 sites.

The golden age of Biblical archeology was led by William Foxwell Albright (1891-1971). He is said to have carried a pick in one hand and a Bible in the other. He used archeology to answer many contemporaries who questioned the Bible's historic reliability. Albright believed the Bible to be infallible. In 1956 Werner Keller, a German journalist, documented many of Albright's discoveries in his book, *"The Bible as History"*. The book sold over ten million copies.[12]

William F. Albright was once a liberal archeologist who attempted to disprove the Bible using archeology. As he dug he discovered that the Bible was extremely accurate.

Albright concluded, *"We no longer trouble ourselves with attempts to harmonize religion and science, or to prove the Bible. The Bible stands for itself."*

Fellow archeologist William M. Ramsay, professor of humanity at the University of Aberdeen, Scotland is considered to be the world's most eminent authority on the geography and history of ancient Asia Minor. He was a Biblical skeptic who after years of investigating the Bible's historic accuracy, went on to write, *"The Bearing of Recent Discovery on the Trustworthiness of the New Testament."* In this work he expressed his admiration of Luke whom he considered to be *"A historian of first rank."* Ramsay went on to say, *"I take the view that Luke's history is unsurpassed in trustworthiness."* Luke specifically names eleven confirmed leaders such as Herod, Caesar, Augustus, and Quirinius. Luke also includes more than 140 details which have been historically proved beyond any doubt.

There has not been one historical detail in the New Testament that has been disproven. In Matthew, Mark, Luke, John, James, and Paul we have six eye witnesses of Jesus Christ who changed their beliefs. Every one of them refused to recant their testimony even under the threat of death. This fact alone would convict anyone in any court of law. It is simply unreasonable to dismiss the Bible as just a fairy tale without historic proof. The Bible is by far the most investigated and proven book ever written.[13]

Sodom and Gomorrah once were thought to be cities that only existed in legend. During excavations from 1975-1981, Walter R. Rast and Thomas Schaub excavated the principle site of Bāb Edh-Dhrā' . They found more than 20,000 tombs where more than 500,000 people were buried. The foundations of the buildings were buried under tons of rubble under which there is clear evidence of a fiery conflagration.

One of the most unique archeological findings clearly supporting the historic accuracy of the Bible was found by Adam Zertel in 1980. He excavated land on Mt. Ebal where he uncovered the altar built by Joshua some 1400 years before Jesus Christ. It was 9 ft. high, 25 ft. wide, and 30 ft. long. Its stones were uncut and the altar had a ramp leading up to it instead of the common steps of similar Pagan altars. (Joshua 8:30-31) *"Joshua built an alter unto the Lord God of Israel in Mt. Ebal...an altar of whole stone, over which no man hath lift up any iron."*

There have been Biblical skeptics who believe that King David was more like King Arthur than a literal king, but in the summer of 1983 one of the most fascinating discoveries was made just a few hundred yards from the southern wall of Jerusalem's old city. Twenty-six clay seals were unearthed bearing the names of King David and dating from 600 BC – 800 BC. This would certainly contain the time of the presumed rule of King David.[14]

One of the more remarkable findings was discovered in 1968 by archeologists V.Corbo and S.Loffreda. They discovered an octagonal shaped building near the Capernaum Synagogue which was one of the earliest Christian churches. The building contained writings on its plastered walls that claimed it was the home of St. Peter. As they continued to excavate they realized the octagon shaped building was built over a house which dated back to the first century, meaning it was most likely the home of St. Peter.[14]

Some of the most publicized discoveries found in Jerusalem over the years have been ossuaries. Ossuaries are the boxes which contained the remains of family members. During the building of a water park in 1990, workers uncovered a Jewish burial cave with 12 ossuaries including the ornate ossuary of Caiaphas, the high priest during Jesus' life. In the November/December 2002 issue of *"Biblical Archaeological Review"*, it was reported that Jesus' family burial cave was found including an ossuary with this inscription, *"James, son of Joseph, brother of Jesus."* The names James, Joseph, and Jesus were very common, but it is unlikely there were a great number of James who also were the son of Joseph, brother of Jesus.[14]

Bruce Feiler had the wonderful idea to read the Pentateuch in the locations in which they were written resulting in his book, *"Walking the Bible; A Journey by Land through the Five Books of Moses"*. Feiler was guided by Avraham Biran, dean of Biblical archeology in Jerusalem and Avner Goren, Israel's chief archeologist and preserver of antiquities from 1967-1982. The Bible is rooted in actual places, not in some far away imaginary land.[15]

Fieler begins his journey between the Tigris and Euphrates, thought to be near the Garden of Eden and widely viewed as the cradle of civilization. From there they traveled to Mt. Ararat where the Bible says Noah's ark landed as the flood waters receded. The flood is the source of ridicule for Biblical skeptics who scoff at the idea of a world-wide flood, even though every civilization on earth has a story of a world-wide flood, and all of the earth was at one time covered by water.

Many of these same skeptics of the Biblical flood have no problem accepting that Mars, which has no water anywhere, was once flooded. While it is difficult to understand those who can't conceive of a world-wide flood, it is certainly easier to understand those who question an ark filled with every animal on earth. Even the most convinced Christian must admit Noah's Ark is a far-fetched idea. However, the Bible goes into great detail to present us with the ark's exact dimensions and the numbers of clean and unclean animals placed into the ark. John Witcomb suggests that the ark had to be large enough to hold at least 3,700 mammals, 8,600 birds, and 6,300 reptiles, approximately 19,000 animals. Witcomb concludes that the average animal is about the size of a small sheep. The Ark could easily hold over 100,000 sheep. Noah'sark may seem improbable but it is not impossible.[15]

The next place visited by Fieler is Hebron, where Abraham is said to have buried his wife Sarah. Today you can visit the incredible memorial built by Herod the Great over the actual burial caves hidden beneath the marble floor. This exact place has been regarded as a holy site for over 3,000 years and there is little doubt that Sarah, Jacob, Isaac, and Rebekah are buried here. (Gen 23:19) *"Abraham buried Sarah his wife in the cave of the field of Machpelah before Mamre: the same is Hebron in the land of Canaan."* It is amazing to read the detail with which the Bible describes exactly where Abraham buried Sarah, and that this burial cave can be visited 3,500 years later.

Eliezer Oren, senior archeologist in the Middle East was asked to give the Bible a grade in terms of its archeological accuracy. He replied with, "A++". Following the journey to write his book Fieler said, *"I met so many scholars who not only confirmed the accuracy of the Bible but also reinforced its beauty."*[15]

One of the most influential events in the Bible and in Jewish culture is the bondage of Israel in Egypt, and the account of how Moses led the Israelites out of Egypt. Liberal historians doubt the entire exodus story because there is little evidence of it in Egyptian writings. This may seem odd but imagine that the Bible describes what happened in light of Egypt's power and pride. Would Egyptian leaders record such an embarrassing event as allowing a group of slaves to walk right out of Egypt?

Even today much more is spoken about George Washington in America than in England. There is no doubt that the Jews recorded much more about the exodus than the Egyptians would have. This is not to say that there is nothing recorded about the Israelites in Egypt, as there certainly is. There were a group of people known as the Hyksos, who were Canaanites and probably included the Israelites.

Another hint as to Israel's presence in Egypt is the fact that the Bible uses many words which have Egyptian origins. The Bible often mentions cows, animals which are not native to Israel but are abundant in Egypt.

Egyptian art does depict stories of a foreigner rising to power in Egypt. Curiously Amenhotep IV radically changed the state of religion in Egypt when he demoted all of Egypt's gods including Amen-Ra, the sun God, and elevated the god Aten as Egypt's one and only God. Some Biblical historians suggest that perhaps Joseph had influenced this change.

Historian Ahmed Osman proposed another idea in his book, *"Stranger in the Valley of the Kings"* where he suggested that Joseph was Yuya, Akhenaten's mysterious grandfather. Yuya seems to come out of nowhere and rises to second in command under King Thutmose IV.

Another indication of the Bible's historical accuracy is found in the very name *"Moses",* which is the Egyptian word for child.

The Bible is Historically True.

Moses is the root word of many Egyptian leaders including Ramses, or Ramoses, and Thutmose. The fact that Moses was raised in Egypt may also explain his hesitance to speak to the Israelites, as he may have had a difficult time speaking Hebrew. This may be why he asked his brother Aaron to be his spokesman.[15]

Many wonder what the Israelites may have built in Egypt while in slavery. Many love to imagine that they helped build the pyramids, but this is unlikely, as the pyramids were probably built much earlier. The Bible tells us exactly what the Israelites were building in Moses' day. (Exodus 1:11) *"They built for Pharaoh the treasure cities, Pithom and Raamses."* Fieler searched for the cities Pithom and Raamses and found ancient cities made up of mud brick houses like the ones recorded in Exodus.

These cities are on the eastern perimeter of the delta and are probably close to where Moses led the Israelites across the Red Sea. These mud brick houses date to 1279 BC-1214 BC, which would place their creation around the time of Ramses II, long considered Egypt's greatest pharaoh.

Interestingly, Ramses II's son Merenptah erected a victory stela describing a great Egyptian victory over the Israelites. This victory stela is one of very few places in Egypt that actually mention the Israelites by name. The problem is that the stela describes a great Egyptian victory instead of a great Israelite escape. Imagine the consequences of a great pharaoh losing thousands of slaves. How else could he explain their sudden absence but the account of a great military victory...?[15]

Of all the sites visited by Fieler, St. Catherine's Basilica is the most remarkable. First, it sits at the base of Mt. Sinai and was built during 542-551 AD on the site where Empress Helena claimed that Moses encountered the burning bush. On the monastery property you can find the Chapel of the Burning Bush. The Church of the Transfiguration also located there is said to have the oldest continually functioning doors in the world, leading into the world's oldest continually operating church. For nearly 1,500 years three services were held every day in the same place, in the same language, and in the exact same manner, numbering nearly three million services.

The monastery also has the second most important collection of religious manuscripts in the world, only bested by the collection housed at the Vatican. There are two prize manuscripts found at St. Catherine's Basilica. The first is the Codex Sinaiticus which is the oldest complete edition of the Bible and the second is the Codex Syriacus, one of the earliest texts of the four gospels from the time that they were first translated into old Syrian in the fifth century.

St. Catherine's Basilica is one of the most remote places on earth which explains why, that despite its amazing history and collection, it is visited by fewer than 10,000 people per year. This is actually a dramatic increase, as there had probably been less than 10,000 visitors in its first 1,200 years of existence.[15]

Mt. Nebo is the single most important Biblical sight in Jordan. It was here that Moses was able to see into the Promised Land after 40 years of wandering in the desert. (Deut.32:49) *"Get thee up into this mountain, unto Mt. Nebo which is in the land of Moab that is over against Jericho; and behold the land of Canaan, which I give unto the children of Israel for a possession."* Holy buildings have existed on Mt. Nebo since the first century BC. The first Christian building on Mt. Nebo was built in 394 AD but was abandoned in 1564 AD. In 1933 the site was excavated, the church was rebuilt and it can be visited to this day.[15]

 Bruce Fieler ends his walk through the Bible with these thoughts: *"The Bible has an amazing ability to unite people in a way nothing else can. The Bible forms kinships greater than nationality, politics, age, or wealth can. The Bible is much deeper than mere faith or science. It has something to say to 5th century monks, 19th century archeologists, and 21st century authors."*[15]

 Fieler continues: *"The Bible is not an abstraction in the Middle East, nor even just a book; it's a living breathing entity undiminished by the passage of time. Its text is forever applicable, it's always now. The Bible makes itself relevant to anyone who encounters it. It has undergone the most concentrated and ruthless academic scrutiny that any written book has ever faced. But in every case (at least those involving historical events), the Bible not only withstood the inquisition but came out stronger, with its integrity intact. The Bible lives today not because it's untouchable but precisely because it has been touched, it has been challenged and it remains undefeated. The Bible has an amazing ability to thrive, even in a world dominated by skepticism."*[15]

The historic accuracy concerning Jesus: Did Jesus exist? Jesus Christ is unique in all of human history. Jesus is so unique that many have a hard time understanding that he actually walked the earth. Jesus is a real historic person whose life is more documented than any other person who has ever been born. In fact, even if you do not include any Biblical accounts of Jesus' life, you could find every detail of his life documented. There are several non-Christian writers who mention Jesus within 150 years of his life. Celsus, Tacitus, The Jewish Talmud, and of course Josephus who writes this about Jesus:

"At the time of Pilate there was a wise man who was called Jesus. His conduct was good and was known to be virtuous. And many people among the Jews and other nations became his disciples. Pilate condemned him to be crucified and to die, but those who had become disciples did not abandon his discipleship. They reported that he had appeared to them 3 days after his crucifixion, and that he was alive; accordingly he was perhaps the Messiah, concerning whom the prophets have recounted wonders." Even without the New Testament there is adequate historical evidence to believe Jesus lived, died, and was believed to have risen from the dead by his disciples.[16]

Bill O'Reilly recently wrote a book, "Killing Jesus" on the life and death of Jesus Christ from an historical and political prospective. While writing, he discovered that there was an enormous amount of historical documentation describing the life and death of Jesus, more than the great Cleopatra, Alexander the Great, and more than all Roman Caesars. The Gospel's account of the life of Jesus is detailed and extremely accurate. Jesus was born during the reign of Caesar Augustus, whose very title speaks to his belief that he was the son of God.

King Herod ruled over Judea at Jesus' birth. He was cruel and demented, killing anyone who threatened his throne. In fact, he killed his own sons who may have desired the throne. The gospel's account of King Herod slaughtering babies upon hearing news of a coming Messiah fits the historical account as to the type of ruler Herod was. Herod's son, Archelaus took the throne when Herod died but did not rule long after killing thousands of Jewish pilgrims during Passover. Rome stepped in, exiled Archelaus to Gaul and stepped up their presence in Judea, making it a Roman province. Caesar Augustus attempted to balance the needs of Rome while keeping the Jewish leaders as happy as possible. He sent Pontius Pilate to be Roman Governor over Judea in the hope that he could keep the peace there.[17]

Pilate was a member of the equestrian class with high aspirations and must have been discouraged in his appointment as Governor of Judea. He did not like the Jews, and attempted to establish his authority by flooding Jerusalem with Roman Standards to remind the Jews of Rome's great power.

The Jews rioted, refusing to allow any graven images near the temple. Pilate begrudgingly relented and removed the Roman Standards. Pilates' rule appeared shaky at best, but he soon formed a powerful and extremely lucrative alliance with Caiaphas, the high priest, who was held in high esteem in Jerusalem. Few people realized the same man who lead the right of atonement of sins had also become a dear friend of Rome. Together they applied several temple taxes as well as money exchanges, making them both very wealthy. The high priests had always been puppets of Rome prior to Caiaphas, but with his political savvy and Pilates' desperate need for an ally in Jerusalem, the two became a powerful force both politically and economically. As a result of this alliance the Jewish leaders enjoyed great economic success. This caused an enormous chasm between religious leaders and the common Jew.

Caesar Augustus also established the four Tetrarchs, appointing Jews to help rule Judea, and three of the four were sons of King Herod. They did wield some power but everyone understood

Pilate had the ultimate authority in Judea. Jerusalem was ruled by temple high priests and the Sanhedrin, which consisted of 71 judges who had authority over any and all religious matters, and Pilate was happy to grant them this power.[17]

The political climate in Jerusalem during the life of Jesus was certainly complex and the gospels portray this complexity in great detail. In AD 14 Caesar Augustus died and Tiberius Caesar rose to power. Tiberius ruled from the Island of Capri, where he was isolated from the everyday chaos in Rome. He enjoyed a life full of sexual perversion as well as delighting in torturing anyone unfortunate enough to get in disfavor. Despite his degenerate lifestyle he had great respect for the Jewish faith. He ordered that the Jews be free to attend any and all feasts and festivals without impediment from Rome. Pilate as well as Herod understood the importance of keeping the peace in Judea.[17]

The money changers converted Roman coins, engraved with the images of past and present rulers and military leaders into shekels. Shekels were the only coin accepted in the temple. The rate was typically four to one. Once the money was converted, the worshiper could use shekels to pay the temple tax and purchase animals for sacrifice. Within the temple walls were massive vaults filled with coins from all over the civilized world. The temple took this money and loaned it out, charging exorbitant interest rates. Both Pilate and Caiaphas profited greatly from this and made certain everything went smoothly as it was of vital importance to all involved.[17]

The Jewish Holy days were vital to the financial well-being and stability of Jerusalem and all of Judea. The common Jew, while full of pride at being part of God's chosen people and understanding the spiritual importance of the feasts and festivals held at the temple, despised the temple tax, the money changers, and the high interest rates on loans. They despised the presence of Roman soldiers on every corner, and they especially despised the tax collectors, primarily Jews who were in effect traitors, getting rich off their own people. They longed for the promised Messiah to come, take the throne in Jerusalem and eliminate the pesky Romans. That was the world Jesus inhabited.[17]

Jesus spent most of his life in obscurity. While there are many opinions as to what Jesus did, the Gospels are silent as to Jesus' life until he is baptized by John the Baptist in the Jordan River.

Once baptized, he wandered in the desert, tempted by Satan for 40 days. He emerged from the desert and chose twelve men who became his Apostles, and followed him all over Judea as he taught and healed the sick. (Matt.4:18-20) *"And Jesus, walking by the Sea of Galilee, saw two brethren, Simon called Peter, and Andrew his brother, casting a net into the sea: for they were fishers. And he saith unto them, Follow me, and I will make you fishers of men.* "Of the twelve Apostles, the majority were fishermen, including Peter who became the leader.

Many have wondered why Jesus chose fishermen to become his disciples. One of the interesting qualities of most fishermen throughout Galilee was their ability to speak many languages. Most fishermen in Galilee could speak Aramaic, Hebrew, Greek, and Latin, needing to speak multiple languages to sell fish. They needed this skill later to become effective fishers of men throughout the Roman Empire. Jesus used the small fishing village of Capernaum as his headquarters for most of his earthly ministry.[17]

How did Jesus' ministry threaten the Pharisees, Sadducees, and even the High Priest Caiaphas? There were probably hundreds of other Rabbis who had large followings, and none of those seemed to bother the Jewish leaders. When we read the Gospels account of Jesus life, it does not seem to describe someone who was trying to grab political power, financial gain or military might, so what threatened the Jewish leaders?

Jesus' disciples' sincerely believed that Jesus was indeed the Messiah. (Matt. 16:13-17) *"When Jesus came into the coasts of Caesarea Philippi, he asked his disciples, saying, whom do men say that I the son of man am? And they said, some say that thou art John the Baptist: some, Elias; and others, Jeremias, or one of the prophets. He saith unto them, But whom say ye that I am? And Simon Peter answered and said, Thou art the Christ, the son of the living God. And Jesus answered and said unto him, blessed art thou..."* It is clear that the disciples understood Jesus to be the Messiah, God's son.

Even the common Jew had begun to see Jesus as the Messiah. I'm certain the Jewish leaders would have believed that God would have notified one of them about Jesus being the Messiah and not a group of fishermen. This is what first brought them to listen to Jesus. If Jesus was the Messiah, then he would certainly consult with them since they were God's representation on earth, or so they believed. However Jesus seemed to deliberately ignore them. This concerned the Jewish leadership.

Jesus claimed to forgive sins. (Matt. 9:2-5) *"And, behold, they brought to him a man sick of the palsy, lying on a bed: and Jesus seeing their faith said unto the sick of the palsy; Son, be of good cheer, thy sins be forgiven thee. And, behold certain of the scribes said within themselves, this man blasphemeth. And Jesus* *knowing their thoughts said, wherefore think you evil in your hearts? For whether is easier, to say, Thy sins be forgiven thee; or to say Arise, and Walk? But that ye may know that the Son of Man hath Power on earth to forgive sins."* One would think that Jesus' amazing miracles would get the Jewish leaders attention, but it was his claim to forgive sins that bothered the Pharisees and Sadducees. Why? They knew that God alone had the power to forgive sins.

They also believed that the only way to get to God was through them. If Jesus somehow by-passed them, no one would need them any longer. This obviously concerned them greatly.

Jesus taught with great authority and used this authority to see through their hypocrisy, often speaking out against the Jewish leadership directly. (Matt 23:13-33) *"But woe unto you, scribes and Pharisees hypocrites! For ye shut up the Kingdom of Heaven against men: For ye devour widows houses and for a pretense make long prayer: therefore ye shall receive the greater damnation. Woe unto you, ye blind guides. Woe unto you, scribes and Pharisees, hypocrites! For ye pay tithe of mint and anise and cumin, and have omitted the weightier matters of the Law, judgment, mercy, and faith. Ye blind guides, which strain at a gnat, and swallow a camel...Ye serpents, ye generation of vipers, how can ye escape the damnation of Hell?* If people ever found out that the Jewish leaders were just as sinful as the common Jew, why would they lift them up as some sort of spiritual hero?

Jesus was teaching that everyone is equally guilty of sin and in need of God's forgiveness, and that he could forgive them, unlike the Jewish leaders who had no ability or willingness to forgive the sins of the common Jew.

Jesus claimed to be God's Son. Here are a few instances in the gospels where Jesus claims to be God's son. Jesus claims to be God's Son as early as age twelve. (Luke 2:48-50) *"And when they saw him, they were amazed: and his mother said unto him, son, why hast thou thus dealt with us? Behold, thy father and I have sought thee sorrowing. And he said unto them how it that ye sought me is? Wist ye not that I must be about my Father's business?"*

Here Jesus claimed to be the fulfillment of Isaiah's prophecy in his hometown. (Luke 4:16-20) *"And he came to Nazareth, where he had been brought up: and, as his custom was, he went into the synagogue on the Sabbath day, and stood up for to read. And there was delivered unto him the book of the prophet Esaias. And when he had opened the book, he found the place where it is written, The Spirit of the Lord is upon me, because he hath anointed me to preach the gospel to the poor; he hath sent me to heal the brokenhearted, to preach deliverance to the captives, and recovering of sight to the blind, to set at liberty that are bruised...And the eyes of all them that were in the synagogue were fastened on him."*

Upon hearing this many were offended and they kicked Jesus out of his own hometown. (John 5:18-24) *"The Jews sought the more to kill him, because he not only had broken the Sabbath, but said also that God was his father, making himself equal to God. Then answered Jesus and said unto them Verily, Verily, I say unto you, The Son can do nothing of himself, but what he seeth the father do...For the Father loveth the Son...For as the father raiseth up the dead, and quickeneth them; even so the son quicketh whom he will...All men should honour the Son, even as they honour the Father."* [18]

It is clear that Jesus claimed to be God's son. In fact it was this act of blasphemy that ultimately sent Jesus to the cross. (Mark 14:61-63) *"Again the High priest asked him, Art thou the Christ, the son of the blessed? And Jesus said I AM: and ye shall see the son of man sitting on the right hand of power, and coming in the clouds of Heaven. Then the High priest rent his clothes, and saith what need we any further witnesses?"*

Many skeptics today say that Jesus was a charismatic teacher and never claimed to be the Son of God. If this were true then why would the Jewish leadership feel so threatened by one charismatic teacher? Jesus clearly claimed to be God's son. Not only did the Gospels record that Jesus claimed to be Messiah, other sources like Josephus recorded that Jesus was thought by his followers to be the Messiah. Claiming to be God was blasphemous and could never be retracted. Jesus was a clear threat to Jewish leadership.

While Jesus may have threatened the Jewish religious leaders like the Pharisees and Sadducees, he posed no threat to Rome until the week before Passover when he once again claimed to be the Messiah. He rode into Jerusalem on a donkey, being worshiped by the crowd who cried, "Hosanna, Hosanna, Hosanna" hoping that this would be the time Jesus would take the throne in Jerusalem and cast the Romans out of Jerusalem for good.

Jesus walked up to the temple and was angry when he saw all the money changers. He turned over the tables, sending coins all over the floor. The Roman soldiers were alerted and Jesus became an unwanted distraction. For the first time Jesus had given Rome a reason to arrest him. However, with such a large crowd filled with those who support Jesus, arresting him became highly risky.[19]

Jesus did not stop. He became openly antagonistic toward the temple authorities as he railed at the hypocrisy of the Jewish leaders. Some of the Pharisees in attendance approached him, trying to trick him by asking if it is right to pay taxes to Rome. This seemed to be a no win question. If he said yes he appeared to support the Roman presence, if he said no then he seems to be encouraging rebellion against Rome. Jesus brilliantly answers, *"Render unto Caesar what is Caesar's and to God what is God's"*. Jesus may have outwitted the Pharisees again, but now it became obvious to them that Jesus must be arrested, tried, and executed, preferably before Passover.

Caiaphas finally had enough evidence to arrest Jesus, but because Jesus was so popular arresting him would be difficult. While Caiaphas and other religious leaders were seeking ways to get rid of Jesus, Jesus' disciples were anxiously awaiting the time when Jesus would make his move and claim the throne in Jerusalem. One of Jesus' closest disciples, Judas Iscariot, saw an opportunity to cash in on his close relationship with Jesus Christ.

Judas had grown tired of waiting for Jesus to make his move and at this point doubt had crept in. What if Jesus was not the Messiah? What if he never takes the throne? Judas had come up with a fool proof plan to expedite things. He knew how badly Caiaphas wanted Jesus arrested, so he would lead the temple guards to Jesus and away from the crowds for the considerable price of thirty pieces of silver, equivalent to four months wages for an average worker of that time. If Jesus was indeed the Messiah he would be forced to reveal his identity in order to avoid arrest. If Jesus was not the Messiah, then Judas would not walk away empty-handed.[19]

Jesus clearly knew this would be the last time he would meet with his disciples before his crucifixion, so he planned what would be known as the last supper. They rented a room on the second floor near the pool of Siloam, a place you can still visit today. As the disciples entered Jesus washed their feet, a task normally reserved for servants. One of Jesus' last lessons for his disciples was to illustrate that the best way to lead people is to serve them first. After he washed the disciples' feet they began their Passover meal. Here Jesus revealed Judas as his traitor and Judas left to make plans to have Jesus arrested.[19]

This was not an ordinary Passover meal. Jesus took this time to prepare his disciples for his coming arrest, trial, crucifixion, and ultimate resurrection. He instituted a way of remembrance not only for those present, but for the billions who would follow. (Luke 22:19-20) *"And he took bread, and gave thanks, and brake it, and gave it to them, saying, this is my body which is given for you: this do in remembrance of me. Likewise also the cup after supper, saying, and this cup is the new testament in my blood, which is shed for you."*

Jesus understood exactly what he was about to do. It was the reason he left heaven to come to Earth. He gave his life as a perfect sacrifice for the sins of all of mankind. Some skeptics believe that Jesus was simply misunderstood, that He never claimed to be God, or correlated His death with a way of forgiving sin. They say his disciples simply made it all up. My question would be why? Why devise a story that so offended the religious leaders of the day that they would hunt down anyone proclaiming Jesus Christ as Savior and kill them? Making this up had no advantages whatsoever. They did not make money or gain political power but instead were hunted and killed. This is not reasonable. The obvious truth is that Jesus must have indeed been God's Son who clearly understood the importance of his dying on an old rugged cross.

After they finished the Last Supper, Jesus led them out of Jerusalem to the Mount of Olives where Jesus went into the Garden of Gethsemane to pray. He asked the disciples to watch and pray as he prayed. They promptly fell asleep and Jesus woke them a couple of times. It is here in the Garden of Gethsemane that it became clear that Jesus understood the gravity of what was about to take place. Jesus, being God, of course knew exactly what must happen.

This has caused many religious scholars to ponder what Jesus was praying for in the Garden of Gethsemane. Notice what Jesus prays, (Luke 22:42) *"Father, if thou be willing, remove this cup from me: nevertheless not my will, but thine be done."* Here are a few thoughts about why Jesus prayed these words. I remember reading this passage as a teenager and asking myself why Jesus seemed so afraid there. There are stories after stories where someone is tortured for their beliefs. The story of Braveheart comes to mind. In each case it seems as though the martyr takes the torture with dignity, courage, and boldness. Why was it that Jesus seemed to be backing out, or at least having second thoughts? This does not seem heroic or brave at all. We must understand exactly what it was that Jesus was dreading here. It was not the physical abuse and pain that he would endure. There were thousands who suffered crucifixion and millions more who also endured severe torture and pain. Most of Jesus' disciples would be tortured and killed just as severely as Jesus would be, and none seemed to express the kind of emotion Jesus was experiencing in the Garden of Gethsemane.

Jesus clearly understood what would happen as he hung on the cross, and it is something beyond our comprehension. It would be on the cross where Jesus would take the cup of man's sin and drink it. Jesus would become sin, taking all of our sin and shame, and he would take the punishment we deserve so that we never have to.

Many people ask why the God of the Old Testament is always smiting people and bringing down judgment on sinful man, yet in the New Testament God seems to be more loving and forgiving. The answer is Jesus. Jesus makes all the difference. It is on the cross where Jesus takes our sin and God turns his back on his only son and punishes the sin. Imagine all of God's wrath and power coming down on his only son. You see, Jesus took the punishment, the wrath of God, the guilt and all the shame on himself as he hung on the cross. Understand that Jesus had lived for eternity past with his father God in Heaven and they had never been separated, but on the cross as Jesus took the cup of man's sin, God would forsake his own son.

It is because Jesus took our sin and God punished that sin as he turned his back on his only son. God poured out all his wrath on Jesus as he hung on the cross, that no one who walks this earth will ever experience even one second apart from the love of God. Think about the Old Testament stories of God's wrath as he poured it on Sodom and Gomorrah, on the worshipers of Baal, and during the great flood when God wiped out all living things except one family and a couple of each kind of animal.

Now think about the kind of wrath and power God must have poured onto Jesus as he took our sins upon him. Why? The answer is because God loves you. (John 3:16) *"For God so loved the world that he gave his only begotten Son, that whosoever believeth in him should not perish, but have everlasting life."*

When you understand all that Jesus must have been thinking about as he poured sweat as blood from his brow, it simply boggles the mind. There is not enough that could be written to adequately express all that Jesus was going through as he prayed and hung on the cross. However, it is important to understand the implications here. Jesus prayed to his Father who loved him so much and asks him if there is any other way for man to be redeemed. If God did not step in with some other plan then it is clear that the only way on heaven or earth for man to be saved is through the precious blood of Jesus Christ.

People often accuse Christians of being narrow minded in believing that there is only one way for sinful man to be saved. If there was any other way for man to be saved, do you not think God would have said so here? The truth is there is no other way. No one else in the history of the world ever lived a perfect life, took man's sin, was nailed to a cross, died and was buried, and three days later rose from the dead. No one else has even claimed to be able to do these things.

As Jesus left the Garden of Gethsemane he was met by a group of temple guards who were led by Judas Iscariot to Jesus. As Judas kissed Jesus the guards arrested Jesus and began one of the most illegal trials ever held. If Jewish law is to be followed then Jesus' trial must wait until morning and a mandatory day of reprieve be given before execution is to be carried out. If this law had been followed, it would have been after Passover before Jesus could be executed, as according to Jewish law no one can be executed during Passover.

The actions of the next 24 hours were unprecedented. Jesus was taken to the house of Anna, Caiaphas' father-in-law, where he was interrogated. Everything about Jesus' interrogation was illegal. First of all it took place at night, Jesus was given no lawyer, and no one present had any authority to pass judgment. As they interrogated Jesus, he remained silent until he was asked if he was God's son, where he answers. (Mark 14: 62) *"I am; and ye shall see the son of man sitting on the right hand of power, and coming in the clouds of Heaven."* Upon hearing this, the high priest Caiaphas ripped his robe and basically says there was no need to continue as it was clear that Jesus was guilty of blasphemy.

When those attending voted, all but Nicodemus found him guilty. As morning broke, the Sanhedrin took Jesus before Pilate to have him executed. When it was revealed that Jesus was from Galilee, Pilate used this as a loophole to remove himself from what would have been a politically tricky decision. Pilate sent Jesus to King Herod Antipas who ruled over Galilee. Herod was delighted to finally meet Jesus but after having John the Baptist decapitated, he was hesitant to execute another Holy man. Herod asked Jesus to prove his deity, and when Jesus fails to do so Herod has him beaten and ridiculed but refuses to execute Jesus.[19]

Caiaphas brought Jesus back before Pilate who questioned Jesus but found no reason to execute him. Caiaphas was adamant about having Jesus crucified but Pilate was reluctant, partly because of his lucrative relationship with Caiaphas. Pilate handled the delicate situation by devising a way to appease Caiaphas and avoids making a religious martyr out of Jesus. It is customary to release a prisoner during Passover, so Pilate sent for the most notorious convict in prison, Barabbas. He then gave the crowd a choice: they could release Barabbas, or Jesus. Unknown to Pilate was the fact that the crowd was made up of Pharisees and Sadducees who desperately wanted to get rid of Jesus, so much so that they would rather free a notorious criminal than free Jesus.

Their response surprised Pilate, who was forced to release a dangerous criminal and crucify an innocent man. Pilate famously washed his hands of the whole incident as Jesus was led away to the cries of *"Crucify Him, Crucify Him..."* [19]

Was Jesus crucified and did he die? It was almost 9 A.M. on a Sunday morning when Jesus was led away to be crucified. The head officer known as the exactor mortis held a sign to be nailed above Jesus on the cross that read, *"Jesus the Nazarene: King of the Jews"* written in charcoal by Pilate himself. It was written in three languages, Greek, the language of the educated, Aramaic, the language of the common man, and Latin, the language of the law.

The sign went before a beaten, bruised, and bleeding Jesus who struggled as he carried a 6 foot unfinished wooden beam weighing nearly 50 pounds a half mile up the hill of Golgotha. Along the way Jesus collapsed in exhaustion and Simon of Cyrene was asked to carry the cross the remainder of the way. Once up the hill, Jesus' hands were nailed to the cross beam and he was hoisted up to his feet and lifted onto an eight foot pole in the ground known as the Staticulum. The sign which read, *"Jesus the Nazarene: King of the Jews"* was nailed above his head. His feet were then nailed to the Staticulum in the ground, and for the next three hours Jesus hung on that old rugged cross as the soldiers cast lots for his tunic.[19]

As Jesus hung on the cross there were seven quotes recorded. Interestingly, these seven quotes are found in Psalm 22 and I will deal with most of them later in the prophetic chapter. For now I wish to examine Jesus saying, (John 19:28) *"I thirst"*. While most simply believe Jesus was physically thirsty and was asking for water, there is much more involved. Remember back to the Garden of Gethsemane where Jesus said, (Luke 22:42) *"Father, if thou be willing, remove this cup from me: nevertheless not my will, but thine, be done."* Jesus has now taken on our sin and God is pouring out his wrath on Jesus, and Jesus is saying *"I THIRST"!*

What Jesus was doing was asking was whether there was any more sin to be taken, more punishment to take. If so, bring it! Jesus was no coward; He is not to be pitied as a martyr. He took the cup of our sin and he drank every drop and thirsted for more. Jesus was in control the entire time. He could have refused to be nailed to a cross, he could have demonstrated his authority to Caiaphas, Herod, or Pilate. Instead he chose to take it all--every sin, all our guilt, all our shame, and he received all the wrath of God toward sin so that we who deserve it will never experience God's wrath. What great love! I do not claim to understand it but I certainly believe and receive it. Will you simply choose to accept God's great love today?

At approximately 3 P.M. Jesus cried out, (John 19:30) *"It is Finished", and* Jesus of Nazareth was dead. The Exactor Mortis had to verify Jesus' death, so he thrust a spear in Jesus side to make certain he was indeed dead. It is interesting to note that a common legend says that the Exactor Mortis at Jesus crucifixion was named Longinus, who was so moved at Jesus' crucifixion that he gave his life to Christ and is considered a saint in both the Roman Catholic Church and the Eastern Orthodox Church.

Once death was verified, Jewish law dictated that the body could not remain on the tree during the Sabbath which began at sundown, so the quaternion takes Jesus' body down.

Most criminals who had been crucified were either burnt outside Jerusalem or buried in a mass grave. As the soldiers removed Jesus' body off the cross a wealthy Sadducee, Joseph of Arimethea comes with Pilate's permission to take the body of Jesus to be buried in his family tomb. There was no time to perform the ritual washing and anointing of Jesus' body with oil so they coated Jesus' body with very expensive myrrh to overwhelm the smell. They wrapped Jesus' body tightly in linen and placed him in the tomb.[19]

The tomb was to be guarded by Roman soldiers and a large stone was placed at the entrance of Jesus' tomb at the request of Caiaphas, who feared Jesus' disciples might come to steal Jesus' body. If Jesus were simply a very charismatic teacher or wonderful healer, this would have been a tragic end to a noble man's life. It is doubtful that anyone would even know his name today. However, over 2,000 years after his death, more than two billion people call him Lord. Why? He got up.

Did Jesus really raise from the dead? There are few who doubt that Jesus actually walked the earth. In fact most people readily accept Jesus as a charismatic leader. The problem is that there have been tens of thousands of very charismatic leaders. but none has made the impact that Jesus Christ has made on world history. What is it about Jesus Christ that causes such world-wide devotion?

I often share this with others concerning Jesus. If you want to be rich, I suggest you follow someone like rich like Warren Buffett. If you want to live a healthy life, I suggest that you follow someone like Jillian Michaels. If you want to be risen from death to live an eternal life, there is only one person in all of history who you can follow, and his name is Jesus Christ. All of Christianity rests not on whether or not Jesus lived, nor the wonderful parables he taught, nor the sick that he healed. All of Christianity rests on the fact that Jesus rose from the dead!

The Apostle Paul makes this statement concerning the resurrection of Jesus Christ. (1 Cor.15:13-17) *"But if there be no resurrection of the dead, then is Christ not risen: and if Christ be not risen, then is our preaching vain, and your faith is also vain."* If Jesus was simply a good man who taught with great authority, healed the sick, lived a righteous life and was crucified as a martyr, he would not deserve worshiping, he should be pitied. However, if he was dead and buried only to rise from the dead three days later, that changes everything. That makes him supernatural and that makes him God. If Jesus is indeed God in the flesh, he must be worshiped, and anything less is blasphemy.

So the question becomes: is there real historic evidence that Jesus was crucified, buried, and rose three days later? Skeptics have invented many theories which debunk the resurrection of Jesus, and here I present some of the more popular ones.

1. The hallucination theory: No one doubts the sincerity of Jesus' disciples as they willingly died defending their belief that Jesus rose from the dead, but many propose that Jesus' disciples were simply hallucinating. First of all, it is difficult to imagine a large number of people all hallucinating at the same time. Secondly and more importantly, it does not explain the empty tomb. If Jesus' disciples were hallucinating and spreading news that Jesus had risen from the dead, why didn't the

Romans or Jewish leaders simply produce the body of Jesus? The fact is that there was no body. [20]

2. The wrong tomb theory: Some suggest that Jesus disciples simply went to the wrong tomb. This is highly unlikely because of the great attention given by the Jewish leaders as well as the Roman guards to the security of Jesus' body. Why would the Roman soldiers guard an empty tomb? Even if you accept that it maybe plausible for Jesus' disciples to go to the wrong tomb on their first visit, I would imagine that they would simply search for the correct tomb. If you were to go to a tomb expecting to see the body of a deceased loved one, would you assume that your loved one had risen from the dead or would you search for the tomb that has the body? It seems highly unlikely that the Roman Soldiers, whose lives depended on guarding the body of Jesus, would be guarding the wrong tomb.[20]

3. The swoon theory: This suggests that Jesus never died. Some claim that Jesus was given something to make him appear dead. This is unlikely for several reasons. First, the Jewish leaders who spent so much effort in getting Jesus on the cross would not be satisfied until Jesus was dead. Second, it was widely known that Jesus had been brutally beaten. If he somehow survived the beatings and six hours hanging on a cross he would be in no shape to walk all over Israel for the next forty days, as witnessed by thousands. If the disciples knew Jesus had somehow faked his death, would they be willing to devote their lives trying to convince others he had risen from the dead? Would they have endured such persecution and ultimate death if they had known Jesus had not truly risen from the dead? [20]

4. The disciples stole Jesus' body: This theory is the least likely of them all. Jewish leaders had already assumed that Jesus'

disciples may try to steal his body, so they arranged with Pilate for the body of Jesus to be guarded. Pilate sent Roman guards and rolled a huge stone over the tomb to prevent them from attempting to do so. You must also consider how afraid the disciples were. Only two of them even dared to show up at Jesus' trial and only one at his crucifixion. They were all afraid that they may be arrested and put to death for associating with Jesus. I cannot imagine a group of fishermen who had the ability to sneak by Roman guards, steal Jesus' body, and devote their lives trying to convince the world Jesus had risen from the dead. This is unreasonable. [20]

5. Jesus was never crucified: The Koran teaches that Jesus was never crucified and many historical scholars agree. However, every respectable historian of Jesus' day records the fact that Jesus was indeed crucified. If Jesus was never crucified, why would thousands of people travel across Israel proclaiming Jesus had risen from the dead if he never died? Jesus' crucifixion is one of the most documented events in history. Some propose that Pilate felt strongly about Jesus' innocence yet felt political pressure to get rid of Jesus, and that he actually crucified someone posing as Jesus and let Jesus secretly sneak out of Jerusalem. That would have been extremely difficult accomplish, even for someone like Pilate. Jewish leaders had risked so much to have Jesus sentenced and crucified that they would have no doubt recognized an imposter. Would Jesus' mother Mary not been able to spot an imposter? Remember too that Jesus did not sneak out of Jerusalem after his crucifixion; he appeared to thousands in the forty days after his crucifixion all over Jerusalem.[20]

When you take time to study the history concerning the Bible, it is clear that the Bible is indeed historically accurate.

The Bible is Historically True.

Archeology continues to reveal just how historically accurate
the Bible really is. There is sufficient evidence that points to the
Bible as historically trustworthy.

There will always be skeptics and critics who throw doubt on
the Bible's historical accuracy, but it continues to be proven
accurate and trustworthy. The fact is that it does not matter
what critics claim. What do you believe?

The Bible is scientifically reliable

"If I told you earthly things and ye believe not, how shall ye believe, if I tell you of heavenly things?" (John 3:12)

The Webster dictionary defines science as the state of knowing, knowledge as distinguished from ignorance or misunderstanding; A system of knowledge covering general truths. There is an attempt by historic revisionist to paint a picture that illustrates how the Bible is against scientific thought. In fact anyone who takes a literal interpretation of the Bible is considered to be an uneducated religious zealot. This subtle attack on the Bible's reliability has proven to be extremely effective as fewer people consider the Bible to be relevant anymore.

The Bible is considered by many to be nothing more than an outdated book of morals rather than the word of God. This has caused our generation to be the most Biblical illiterate generation in American history, which has caused many social problems that are only getting worse. I believe the Bible is the most trustworthy book ever written. If you take the time to study the Bible, you will find it to be very consistent with the laws of science. In fact, the Bible is more consistent with the proven laws of science than most of the scientific theories taught in our schools today.

Despite popular opinion, Christians who take a literal view of the Bible are not all religious fanatics who are against science. As a matter of fact those who hold a literal view of the Bible understand that if the Bible is God's Word, then it will align perfectly with scientific law. After all if God created the universe and if God inspired the writers of the Bible, then would you not expect the Bible to be consistent with scientific laws? In this chapter I would like to compare the Bible with many popular scientific theories which are being taught in schools today to see which compares closer to proven scientific laws. I would first like to dismiss the common misconception that is widely accepted today that Christians have historically fought against scientific thought. The truth is the earliest scientist were Bible believing Christians and nearly every college and university in Europe and America were all started by Christians who believed so strongly that the Bible was true in every sense, that they used the Bible as the basis of higher education...including science.

Science originated & higher education was advanced by Bible believing Christians.

Our world today is the most educated generation in all of history largely because of the church which used the Bible to help the common person read and write. The Bible was used to establish most every college and university in America and Europe. The world's oldest English speaking university, Oxford was certainly established by men who held the Bible in high regard. While most students who attend Oxford today may be oblivious to it, Oxford grew out of a monastery as early as 1096. Throughout Oxford's long history it has proven to be deeply rooted by the Bible. Oxford's motto is *"Dominus Illuminatio Mea"* which is Latin for *"The Lord is my Light"* and is taken from Psalm 27. Before any formal meal in the dining hall of one of Oxford's oldest colleges, Merton College, the senior postmaster says grace by repeating this passage from Psalm 145, *"The eyes of the world look up to thee, oh Lord. Thou givest them food in due season. Thou openest thou hand and fillest every creature with thy blessing. Bless us, oh God, with all the gifts which by thy good works we are about to receive. Through Jesus Christ our Lord Amen."* Many of Oxford's graduates have gone on to become great men of God. Men like C.S. Lewis, Author of the Chronicles of Narnia and powerful Christian apologetics writer, John Wesley, founder of the Methodist Church, William Tyndale, & John Wycliffe who both translated the Bible helping it to become the world's best-selling book. It is clear that the Bible has influenced one of the most prestigious universities in the world more than any other book ever written.[1]

Some of America's most respected universities are Harvard, Yale, & Princeton, all three of which were started by men who viewed the Bible as the foundation of higher learning. When you look back at the history of these 3 prestigious universities you can't help but notice how the Bible influenced each of them. Harvard was named after John Harvard, who was a minister of the gospel of Jesus Christ. Harvard's first president was Henry Dunster who was also a minister. In fact Dunster was known for his diligence in studying the Word of God. He felt it was the highest duty of educators to be able to teach Biblical truths. Harvard was founded in 1636, ten years later in 1646 Harvard adopted rules and precepts which would guide the college. Among these rules and precepts were these; 1."*Let every student be plainly instructed, and earnestly pressed to consider well, the main end of his life and studies is to know God and Jesus Christ which is eternal life, and therefore to lay Christ in the bottom, as the only foundation of all sound knowledge and learning. 2. Everyone shall so exercise himself in reading the scriptures twice a day.*

The Bible is Scientifically Reliable.

In 1692 Harvard adopted "VERITAS *Christo et Ecclesiae"* which is Latin for *"Truth for Christ and the Church"*. Is there any doubt that Harvard was established by Christians who considered the Bible to be the cornerstone of higher learning? Ten of Harvard's first twelve presidents were ordained ministers.[2]

On May 6th 1735 William Tennent wanted his sons to receive the best education possible to prepare them for ministry but was disappointed in Harvard and Yale so he constructed a Log house and used it as a school which became known as *"Log College"* . This Log College produced many Presbyterian ministers who were key in America's great awakening. Tennent died in 1746 and the Log College closed its doors only to be opened up again a year later to start a *"Seminary of learning"* with a royal charter for the college of New Jersey which would eventually become Princeton. Most of Princeton's early presidents were Presbyterian ministers including Jonathan Edwards who was considered one of America's most famous evangelists.[3]

In 1951 William F. Buckley Jr. wrote a controversial book *"God and Man at Yale"* where he described how the liberal leadership at Yale had turned away from its Christian founding just as most other universities have done. Yale was started by ten Congregationalists ministers who desired to educate students in the Christian religion. Yale's motto became *"Christ the Word and interpreter of the father, our light and perfection."* This motto was later changed to *"The light of the great awakening and truth of the enlightenment"*. This was changed to simply *"Light and truth"* which is the motto today. Yale as well as Harvard, Princeton, and numerous other liberal universities have totally forgotten the light and truth they were all founded on.[4]

The Bible is Scientifically Reliable.

I challenge anyone to find any other book, philosophy, religion, or government which has impacted higher education more than the Bible. No matter how loud and numerous the critics of the Bible are they can in no way say with any authority that those who take a literal view of the Bible are against higher learning. In fact if it were not for those who saw the Bible as humanities greatest source of truth and understanding, there may have never been a scientific renascence. Modern science has hijacked the truth which is that the most fruitful science that has been done in the past was done by scientist with a Biblical world view. Just look at this short list of scientist who had a Biblical world view.

Sir Isaac Newton was an amazing intellectual, who not only discovered gravity, but developed calculus, & designed the first reflecting telescope. He was quoted as saying *"No sciences are better attested than the religion of the Bible."*[5]

Robert Boyle who is considered to be the father of modern chemistry also published what he considered his greatest work *"The Christian Virtuoso"*. He described the moral responsibility of man to understand and care for the physical world as God commanded in Genesis 1:28.[6]

Louis Pasteur, an outspoken Christian, developed the concept of pasteurization and spent much of his life arguing that Darwin's theory of evolution was absurd as spontaneous generation is unscientific.[7]

Johannes Kepler was a German Astronomer who discovered 3 planetary laws which laid the foundations for Galileo to ultimately conclude that the Sun did not revolve around the earth as the scientific community had believed but the earth revolved around the sun. Kepler believed the natural world reflected the God who created it. One of Kepler's favorite verses of the Bible was (John 1:14) *"And the Word was made flesh, & dwelt among us."* He felt this verse described the close relationship between the natural world & the God who created it.[8]

Gregor Mendel was born in 1822 in Austria. He became a monk and attended the Abbey of St. Thomas in Brunn. The Abbey of St. Thomas was known as a world-wide leader in the teaching of the sciences. The Church, both Catholic and protestant, led the world in educating the world, especially in the sciences from the 16th through the 19th centuries. Mendel seemed much more interested in the sciences than religious studies but even so Mendel became a priest in 1847 but by 1850 he quit to continue his real interest which was the sciences. In 1865 he founded the *Austrian Meteorological society.* Mendel actually published more books on meteorology than on genetics. It was his work on genetics, specifically on the heredity of peas that gained Mendel notoriety.

Mendel meticulously recorded traits of over 30,000 different plants over an 8 year period of time. The results were amazing, but were widely ignored, due to the scientific community's obsession with Darwin's theory of evolution. Mendel's findings concerning genetics did not fit Darwin's natural selection theories as a result it would be nearly 40 years later until Mendel's studies of genetics were found to be quite reliable. Today the study of genetics continues to prove that Mendel's theories on genetics were far more reliable than Darwin's theories of evolution. Unfortunately Mendel's work on genetics is over shadowed by Darwin's theory of evolution, even though Mendel's work is far more reliable.[9]

The Bible is Scientifically Reliable.

French mathematician, physicist, and inventor Blaise Pascal was also an outspoken Christian apologist as he often defended the rationality of the Bible. He famously said *"There is a God shaped vacuum in the heart of every man which cannot be filled by any created thing, but only by God, the creator, made known through Jesus."*[10]

The founder of modern surgery, Joseph Lister was a Bible believing Quaker who helped develop antiseptic surgery which saved thousands of lives. He became the prof. of Clinical surgery at Edinburgh where he faithfully attended the Scottish Episcopal Church.[11]

British Physicist & Chemist, Michael Faraday, was also a lay preacher who believed that all of nature was interconnected as it was created by one God. He believed that electricity & magnetism must be interconnected which enabled him to ultimately invent the electric motor.[12]

Many may say that these forefathers of science were only Christian because nearly everyone claimed to be Christian during the 17th -19th century but there are a growing number of scientist today that are devout Christians. John Polikinghorne who has won many awards for his work in mathematical physics is also an Anglican priest who has written many books on the relationship between science & religion.[13]

Francis Collins who led the human genome project & has received the presidential Medal of Freedom as well as the national medal of science and is currently the director of the National institutes of Health in Bethesda, Maryland. He wrote the New York Times best seller *"The Language of God: A Scientist presents evidence for belief."* Collins entered college claiming to be an atheist but once a doctor who grappled with the death of many of his patients he credits the writings of C.S. Lewis with leading him to Jesus Christ and Collins is considered to be evangelical Christian's most well respected scientist.[14]

Then there is one of the leading scientist in researching climate change, Katherine Hayhoe, who is also the wife of a preacher & is a bit of an enigma as an atmospheric scientist who supports global warming as well as an evangelical Christian. She is one of Time magazine's 100 most influential people of 2014. from a biblical perspective versus an evolutionary perspective.[15]

This is a very short list of Christians who have led the world in scientific thought over the past 500 years. The question I have is why has modern science moved away from God? The simple answer is Darwin. In 1859 Darwin published *On the Origin of Species* which introduced the world to evolution & it gave the scientific community a way to finally get around what many considered the "God" problem. Darwin made it popular to believe the universe came about by chance & not by God. This began a trend in which most scientist today are at best agnostic if not outright atheist.

The problem is, when you rule out any need for God it leaves science having to imagine some far out theories to deal with life's most basic questions like...When, why, & how did the universe begin? How did life originate? How did language originate? Why do we exist? What is our future?...While science seems confounded by these questions the Bible gives us clear, concise, & scientifically reasonable answers to all of these questions and more.[16]

Today's Christian is frequently confronted with the problem of alleged scientific mistakes in the Bible especially when it comes to the story of Creation. This leaves most Christians intimidated by the weight of popular opinion. It has caused today's youth to ignore the Bible & readily accept the world's theories. Jesus demonstrated the importance of God's word to be taken as historic & scientific truth when he said (John 3:12) *"If I told you earthly things & ye believe not, how shall ye believe, if I tell you of heavenly things?"* In other words if you can't believe what the Bible teaches about simple things like science & history why would you accept it as spiritual truth? Understand the Bible is not a scientific text book, it is however scientifically reliable.[16]

Why is it that modern science is so adamant that the Bible can't be considered when dealing with scientific theories yet any word that Stephen Hawking mumbles has liberal professors wetting themselves with excitement? Modern science has spent millions of dollars and countless hours studying the possibility of multiple universes, time travel, string theories, aliens, even zombies may not be out of the question these days...but let someone recommend spending time or money on studying how God may have created the universe, or how a world-wide flood may explain what we find all around the world and they just shake their heads in disbelief.

 Despite an obvious bias against any scientist who has a Biblical world view there is a growing number of scientist who accept the Bible's creation story as being true according to Ken Ham. He keeps a list of these *"Creation Scientist"* on his web page as well as the answers in Genesis web page. I truly believe that as Darwin's theory of evolution begins to lose favor among scientist that more will begin to take an honest look at the Bible's creation story as being the best explanation of creation.[17]

The Bible is Scientifically Reliable.

In Jonathan Sarfati's book *"Refuting Evolution"* he states *"It is wrong to claim that denying evolution is rejecting the type of science that put men on the moon, although many evolutionary propagandists make such claims. Actually the man behind the Apollo moon mission was the creationist rocket scientist Wernher von Braun.".* [18] Sarfati also refutes the misleading idea that the church was against Galileo's scientific discoveries which included that the Earth was a sphere and not flat. It was the scientific establishment of Galileo's day that accepted the Aristotelian/Ptolemaic theory which believed the earth was at the center of the universe and was flat. The Aristotelians at the Universities, not the church, were the first to reject Galileo's theories. While the Roman Catholic Church may have rejected Galileo's theories; one of the leading theologians of the day, Cardinal Robert Bellarmine said Galileo's theories made *"excellent good sense".*

Galileo may have had disputes with the Catholic Church but he continued to hold a Biblical world view. Excerpts from the letter to Madame Christina help to reveal Galileo's view of Scripture and that of his predecessors. He writes, *"I think in the first place that it is very pious to say and prudent to affirm that the Holy Bible can never speak untruth—whenever its true meaning is understood."* [18]

Modern science demands a naturalistic explanation for any and everything we find whether it is how the universe began? Or how did life begin? or Where did man come from? By demanding a naturalistic explanation it automatically excludes any theory which needs a creator. This may sound fair but it is not reasonable. It is like demanding a natural explanation for Mt. Rushmore. If you were asked how Mt. Rushmore was formed you would say that someone carved it and you would be correct. What if someone then told you that there had to be a naturalistic explanation for how Mt. Rushmore was created?

You could no longer use *"the crutch"* that someone carved it. This would force you to leave reason and begin to imagine outrageous theories that could possibly explain how Mt. Rushmore was formed. Maybe over millions of years water carved it, or possibly a volcano erupted, or could it be that tectonic plates shifted causing it to form what appears to be the faces of four presidents. You see how ridiculous it is to force a naturalistic explanation for something that was obviously carved by someone with the intelligence and skill.[19]

This is exactly what modern scientist have done when it comes to life's most basic questions. They have demanded naturalistic explanations for things that were obviously created by an intelligent and skillful creator. Let's compare how the Bible answers the most basic questions concerning creation with what modern science teaches about these same questions and ask yourself which is more reasonable.

How did the universe begin? There are only 3 possible answers to this question. 1. The universe is eternal and it had no beginning. This was the theory widely accepted by scientist and philosophers like Aristotle and Socrates who both viewed the universe as eternal. Christianity caused many to reject the belief of an eternal universe as the Bible obviously describes God creating the universe in Genesis, but the idea of an eternal universe began to gain popularity in the 1920's by Sir James Jean who came up with the steady state theory which was later published by Boni, Gold, and Hoyle in 1948.

The Bible is Scientifically Reliable.

The Steady State Theory states that the universe has always expanded at a uniform rate with no beginning or end. The theory did not last too long as Edwin Hubble began making observations of an expanding universe which was predicted by Einstein's theory of General Relativity in 1915 and which points to the universe having a beginning. The discovery of cosmic microwave background radiation by A.G Doroshkevich and Igor Novikov in 1964 suggests that this radiation is the remnant of the Big Bang. In fact there has been such overwhelming evidence pointing to the universe having a beginning that Alexander Vilenkin, professor of Physics at Tufts University, says *"All the evidence we have says that the universe has a beginning."*[19]

The idea that the universe has a beginning is troubling for atheist as Stephen Hawking admits in this quote from his book, *a brief History of Time, "So long as the universe had a beginning, we could suppose it had a creator."*[20] This is a bold statement which Hawking certainly regrets that he ever said in light of the overwhelming evidence that the universe did have a beginning and is not eternal.[21]

2. The universe somehow, by chance, came into existence. This is now what atheist are holding onto as the best option left in describing the beginning of the universe. It is interesting that the person credited with proposing what would become the big bang theory was a Catholic priest. Georges Lemaitre, professor of physics at the Catholic University of Leuven is credited with proposing what he called his "hypothesis of the primeval atom" which later became known as the Big Bang theory. Russian Cosmologist George Gamow is credited with advancing the Big Bang theory that is widely accepted as the best explanation of the origin of the universe.

The Bible is Scientifically Reliable.

The Big Bang Theory states that the universe began in a hot dense state where primarily light atoms hydrogen and helium clumped together by gravitational attraction to form countless trillions of stars. The big bang theory is widely accepted and can be adopted by both Christians as well as atheist. Christians simply say God spoke and there was a big bang, while atheist can simply accept that the big bang happened naturally by chance with no need of a creator. This has certainly helped the Big Bang Theory gain its overwhelming acceptance by the civilized world, but is it in fact the most scientifically reliable theory?[22]

There are some scientific problems with the big bang theory. Dr. James Trefil, professor of physics at George Mason University, admits *"there shouldn't be galaxies out there at all, and even if there are galaxies, they shouldn't be grouped together the way they are...The problem of explaining the existence of galaxies has proved to be one of the thorniest in cosmology. By all rights, they just shouldn't be there, yet there they sit. It's hard to convey the depth of the frustration that this simple fact induces among scientists."* Dr. John Rankin and Dr. Danny Faulkner also suggest that no stars could form as a result of a big bang. Abraham Loeb of Harvard's center for astrophysics says *"The truth is that we don't understand star formation at the fundamental level."* While the Big Bang theory is widely accepted today it is far from true science. The problem is that no theory concerning the origin of the universe can be truly scientific, because no one observed, recorded, or measured it..[23]

Walt Brown brings up a few problems with the Big Bang, one of which is that distant galaxies appear to be accelerating rather than decelerating as would be expected from a big band billions of years ago. A big bang should not produce highly concentrated group of rotating bodies as we see in thousands of galaxies throughout the universe. Also much of the Universe moves perpendicular to the direction of supposed expansion from a big bang. One would expect a big bang to produce only hydrogen and helium making it highly unlikely for stars to form. Finally if the Big Bang theory is correct then it would make calculating the age of the universe possible. The problem is that it early calculations reveal a much younger universe than evolutionist need to fit their unscientific theories.[24]

Henry Morris also brings up some problems with the Big Bang in his book *"The Biblical basis for Modern Science"*. The universe is full of empty spaces with huge conglomerations of matter scattered around the cosmos. You would expect there to be more uniformity radiating from the supposed Big Bang. It is hard to justify the accumulation of any amount of matter in one location such as a star. How could a great explosion that drives matter apart allow atoms to come together and form stars? If the universe had a chaotic, random, unguided origin & development then isn't it remarkable that the entire universe can be described by the same set of natural laws. In fact it is the predictability of nature that allows for science to occur. If the universe did not always follow certain laws then science would not be effective. One of the great problems that evolutionist have is trying to explain all the order in the universe.[25]

If you choose to accept the big bang theory then let me ask how a huge explosion caused so much order. As a child I loved playing with fireworks & I used to enjoy blowing things up. I must have blown up 100's of ant hills but I must say never once did those explosions ever form anything but a mess. Yet I am told that a huge explosion formed the universe? Not only that but when I say I believe that God created the universe then people say I am the one who is uneducated & foolish when their explanation flies in the face of all logic & reason.

One of the fundamental problems with evolution and the big bang is that they attempt to explain how the universe began under the assumption that everything we see in the universe all began at some point from nothing & grew into what we see today. What if God created the universe in 6 literal days as described in Genesis? What if God simply spoke and the universe came into existence as we observe it today? Could it be that all the stars, planets, moons, and comets all came into existence at God's word... fully grown? This may sound ridiculous but understand the Bible records God forming Adam from the dust of the earth. When you picture Adam, do you imagine a baby or does the Bible suggest that Adam was a fully grown adult?

It is clear to me that Adam never was an infant, he was a fully mature man from day one of his existence. If this is true, then would you not expect that the earth, moon, and sun to be fully mature from day one as well? I believe this explains why scientist will always be confounded when trying to explain the origin of the universe. This also explains why there is scientific evidence that points to a young earth while there is also scientific evidence that points to an extremely old earth. Why? If you mistakenly assume that the Earth was born instead of created fully mature by God then you will get conflicting evidence.[25]

Certainly there is evidence which point to an Earth billions of years old. The oldest known rock on earth according to a study done by McGill University is thought to be 4.28 billion years old.

They are known as the "Faux-amphibolite's" they were discovered by Jonathan O'Neil, a PhD candidate at McGill's Department of Earth and planetary sciences, along the Hudson Bay Coast in northern Quebec. They are believed to be a part of the earth's primordial crust. Since the earth must be older than anything found on it then evidence certainly points to an extremely old earth, at least 4.28 billion years old. When you consider the age of the universe, NASA's Wilkinson Microwave Anisotropy Probe (WMAP) and The European Space Agency's Planck spacecraft have measured the thermal radiation left over from the big bang and determined the universe to be 13.82 billion years old. There are hundreds of other facts that support the idea that the Earth is billions of years old and they are well documented.[26]

There are several facts that seem to support a much, much, younger earth, these facts are seldom referenced or documented but they are real. Here are a few that I found in "In the Beginning, Compelling evidence for creation and the flood" by: Walt Brown PhD

The declining magnetic field. As far back as 1590 sailors have used the magnetic field for navigation. Their records are extremely accurate and steady it shows a steady decline in the magnetic fields strength. If you assume that the Earth's magnetic field decays at this same rate then the Earth could not have supported life 25,000 years ago.[27]

The salt in the oceans. For over 100 years scientists have measured the amount of minerals that are deposited into the oceans as well as the amount of minerals which evaporate from the ocean. 457 tons of salt are deposited every year while 122 tons evaporate, meaning that 335 tons of salt accumulate every year. If you conservatively say that only 100 tons of salt accumulated the oceans would be dry in less than 60 million years...much less than the 4 billion years that most scientist believe the Earth to be. However if you take the rate of 335 tons of salt accumulated yearly and count back you arrive at around 4500 years ago...[27]

Evolutionists date the sun at 4.6 billion years old if this is correct the slowly condensing Sun would have radiated 25-30% less heat than it does today. Understand a drop in the sun's radiation of only a few percent would freeze all the earth's oceans.[27]

Heat always flows from a hot body to a cold body, if the universe were billions of years old then there should not be such extreme temperatures within the universe. Everything should be about the same temperature by now.

Lead diffuses from zircon crystals at known rates that increase with temperature and time. If this is true then you would expect that the deeper you go into the earth's crust the higher temperatures would dictate that there would be little or no lead, yet there is no difference in the amount of lead throughout the top 4000 meters. This indicates the earth is much younger than 4.6 billion years.[27]

The amount of river sediments that are deposited into the oceans has been recorded for almost 100 years and on average the rivers deposit 27 billion tons of sediment into the ocean. At this rate the oceans would be filled in only 30 million years. However if you assume the rate of 27 billion tons of sediment every year is deposited then the rivers have been depositing sediment into the ocean for about 4500 years[27]

The Bible is Scientifically Reliable.

Meteoritic dust which is high in nickel accumulates on the earth each year, if this has happened for 4.6 billion years then you would expect to find high concentrations of nickel on the earth's surface yet none is found which indicates a much younger earth. Scientist agree that the earth was initially molten, if this is true then the earth's core would have cooled off in 4.6 billion years. Yet the earth's core is over 10,000 degrees Fahrenheit. This indicates the earth is much younger.[27]

The moon is moving slowly away from the earth. In 1695 Edmund Halley first observed this phenomenon. If the moon began on earth and it slowly moved away from the earth it would be much farther away from the earth if it travelled 4.6 billion years[2]

Evolutionist often use radiocarbon dating as proof of the world being billions of years old but there have been shocking discoveries by scientist who have studied Mt. St. Helens. Mt. St. Helens erupted in 1980 & scientist were amazed to find carbon which was formed overnight by the extreme heat & force of the eruption. When you measure the age of this carbon they give radiometric ages of 2.8 million years when they were obviously just formed in 1980. This indicates that radiocarbon dating is not very reliable. In fact there are literally 100's of ways to measure the age of the earth & a majority of them point to a much younger earth than evolutionist assume. In fact less than 10% of ways to measure the earths age actually indicate an earth over a billion years old & of course these are the indicators all evolutionist use while they simply ignore the 90% of indicators which point to a much younger earth.[28]

Heat always flows from a hot body to a cold body. If the universe was billions of years old then everything should have the same temperature. The fact that temperatures vary greatly throughout the universe reveals the universe is much younger than evolutionists propose.[29]

Then there is Niagara Falls which sends 6 million cubic ft. of water every minute over the falls which erodes the basin at a rate of 1 meter a year. If the falls eroded at a tenth of this it would have already eroded into Lake Erie thousands of years ago. Yet at the 1 meter rate, the falls date to about 4500 years ago...The reason why Niagara Falls has not eroded much further over millions of years still eludes scientists today.[30]

The best way to take both sets of scientific evidence and make them both fit is to simply take God at his word and understand God created a fully grown universe in 1 day just as he created a fully grown man in 1 day. This would adequately explain how there is evidence of an old earth just like there is a young earth.

3. The universe was designed and created by some great force. *"In the beginning God created the Heavens and the Earth"* (Genesis 1:1) There is no greater theory of the origin of the universe than the one in God's word. It may seem simple but it is by far the most scientifically sound theory we have. The most basic & trusted of all scientific laws is the Law of thermodynamics. Sir Frances Bacon said *"True knowledge is knowledge by causes."* This is why science works. If it were not for the law of causality no one could test any scientific theories. Nothing in all of observable science has ever happened without a cause. The most basic & trusted of all scientific laws is the laws of thermodynamics.

The First Law of Thermodynamics states that neither matter nor energy can be created or destroyed. The amount of energy in the universe is constant – energy can be changed, moved, controlled, stored, or dissipated. However, this energy cannot be created from nothing or reduced to nothing. Every natural process transforms energy and moves energy, but cannot create or eliminate it. This principle forms a foundation for many of the physical sciences. Science has shown that the First Law of Thermodynamics applies to all matter and energy, no matter how much or what the conditions are. Looking at bigger and bigger systems of matter and energy eventually leads to a question: where did all of the matter and energy in the universe come from? The Bible's account of creation fits the most basic of scientific law unlike the many theories that modern scientist have come up with.[31]

The Second Law of Thermodynamics is commonly known as the Law of Increased Entropy. While quantity remains the same (First Law), the quality of matter/energy deteriorates gradually over time. How so? Usable energy is inevitably used for productivity, growth and repair. In the process, usable energy is converted into unusable energy. Thus, usable energy is irretrievably lost in the form of unusable energy.[31]

"Entropy" is defined as a measure of unusable energy within a closed or isolated system (the universe for example). As usable energy decreases and unusable energy increases, "entropy" increases. Entropy is also a gauge of randomness or chaos within a closed system. As usable energy is irretrievably lost, disorganization, randomness and chaos increase.

The implications of the Second Law of Thermodynamics are considerable. The universe is constantly losing usable energy and never gaining. We logically conclude the universe is not eternal. The universe had a finite beginning -- the moment at which it was at "zero entropy" (its most ordered possible state). Like a wind-up clock, the universe is winding down, as if at one point it was fully wound up and has been winding down ever since. The question is who wound up the clock? Again it is the Bible, not modern science that offers a scientifically reasonable answer.[31]

The principles of thermodynamics are regarded by scientists to be the most universal of all the laws of physics yet the theory of evolution goes against the principles of thermodynamics while Biblical creation fits nicely. The Bibles account of creation however agrees totally with the basic principles of science. (Gen 2:1-2) *"Thus the heavens & the earth were finished, & all the host of them. & on the 7th day God ended his work which he had made"* According to the Biblical account of creation, God created all things & once He was finished the act of creation was finished. This is exactly what the 1st principle of thermodynamics says.[31]

The 2nd principle of thermodynamics state that the energy of the universe is decreasing. According to the theory of evolution things are becoming more advanced. Every time something evolves it gets more complex and advanced. If you accept this theory of evolution then you must ignore the 2nd principle of thermodynamics. So once again the majority of modern scientist have willingly ignored basic laws of science in order to explain away a creator God. The Bible is once again in total agreement with the 2nd principle of thermodynamics as it says (Gen 3:17-19) *"Cursed is the ground for thy sake; in sorrow shalt thou eat of it all the days of thy life; thorns also & thistles shall it bring forth to thee; & thou shalt eat the herb of the field; in sweat of thy face shalt thou eat bread, till thou return unto the ground."* The Bible teaches ⁱthat man's sin has cursed the earth & has caused God's perfect creation to slowly die.[31]

The Bible is Scientifically Reliable.

All processes of the universe operate within the framework of the 1st & 2nd laws of thermodynamics. The term thermodynamics is Greek for "heat power" & it speaks to the conversion of heat into work. Once this process was quantified it was soon discovered that the same process used to convert heat to work was true for all conversion processes. Today the Laws of thermodynamics are universally accepted as one of the most fundamental of all scientific laws. The first Law of thermodynamics is also known as the law of conservation which says that energy can be transferred from one place to another or from one form to another. This energy can't be created or destroyed. When applied to the universe it suggests that the total quantity of energy within the universe is constant, nothing is created or destroyed but everything is somehow being conserved. Scientist are baffled as to how this could be possible as it is contrary to everything evolution assumes. It is however uncannily similar to what the Bible teaches.

The 2nd law of thermodynamics stats that no device can deliver work unless there is a difference in energy concentration with the system, no matter how much total energy is used. To put this in layman's terms it simply states that all things decay over time. This is also known as entropy. The rate of decay can be sped up or slowed down but it can never be reversed. This poses a serious threat to the theory of evolution as there must have been an uncaused first cause which created the universe. The only way to escape this conclusion is to leave reality & appeal to evolutionary metaphysics in order to be free from the laws of science. - Which say that nothing in the universe is now being created but is being conserved. All things decay & die. Evolution obviously ignores these basic rules of science while the Bibles account of creation agrees with these most basic laws of science. How is it that those who believe in the Bible which aligns with scientific law are considered uneducated & narrow minded while those who accept evolution which does not.[32]

If the universe had a beginning it must have had a cause. The 2nd law of thermodynamics says that the universe is running out of energy. Ironically, evolutionist have wandered so far away from the basic laws of science that they understand fully that evolution does not now & never will fit into any basic scientific structure so you would assume that they would quit accepting evolution as a viable scientific theory...you would be wrong. Instead of rejecting evolution due to its incompatibility with the basic laws of science evolutionist have simply created an imaginary branch of fairy tale science known as Evolutionary metaphysics.

Here evolutionists can form any & all kinds of theories without trying to fit them into any pesky scientific law. They use complicated mathematical equations to presuppose theories which are all unscientific. Some of the popular evolutionary metaphysical theories are quantum theories which allows for quantum fluctuations of nothing into something which somehow over billions of years just by chance formed this remarkably ordered universe. Then there are theories which describe multiple universes which add even more chances for nothing to somehow evolve into everything. There is also the string theory which excites many physicist today. The string theory suggests that there maybe multiple dimensions or strings within the universe, of course you must leave the real 3 dimensional world of science in order to accept any of these ridiculous theories.[33]

The Bible is Scientifically Reliable.

What amazes me is the audacity the modern scientific community has in looking down at those who take a literal view of the Bible as if we are somehow against science; when the only way to accept evolution is to ignore the most basic and widely understood scientific laws. These modern scientist have used untestable theories and tried to pass them as real science while accusing Bible believing scientist of being unscientific. Unlike modern science, the Bible's creation account follows basic scientific laws of the 1st and 2nd laws of thermodynamics. No other theory currently studied by modern scientist today follows the most understood and proven of all scientific Laws...the 1st & 2nd Laws of thermodynamics.

How did life begin? Evolution teaches that all matter formed from nothing & somewhere, somehow, in an unknown process the first living cell formed in some primeval pool. This single cell evolved over time into a more complex living animal & over time this one kind of animal somehow evolved into different species...does this follow any laws of known science? Also consider the great mystery of consciousness. How is it that non-living life somehow gain consciousness? Evolution accepts that all things happen naturally & that everything is formed from chemicals & matter. However if life is nothing more than a chemical reaction in matter then why is it that scientist have yet to discover how to make something live? There is no chemical difference in a living animal & a dead animal but there is a huge difference ...life. Modern science remains baffled at how consciousness even takes place. Evolution can't properly explain how life began yet it is accepted as scientific truth despite having no scientific support.[34]

The sciences of physics & chemistry are the most understood of all sciences. Chemistry deals with the basic structure of matter as well as reactions between them, while physics deal with the forces & energy exerted by & upon matter. The Bible alludes to these sciences in a couple of interesting ways. It is interesting that the Bible indicates that God used the dust of the earth to form plants, animals, & to create humans. This seems to allude to the scientifically accurate fact that God used the exact same matter, the dust of the earth, to form & create all living things. God used only the elements found on the earth to create everything.

These basic elements are combined in extremely ordered & complex ways to form each living thing on earth. These elements are not random & it is simply not reasonable to assume that these elements by chance formed such advanced, complex, & orderly forms of life. It is far more reasonable to accept the Bibles account that a wise & powerful creator meticulously designed all living things to work perfectly. Also it is interesting to note how the Bible speaks to the elements as being # by weight. (Isaiah 40:12) *"Who hath measured the waters in the hollow of his hand, & metered out heaven with the span & comprehended the dust of the earth in a measure & weighed the mountains in scales & the hills in a balance?"* The Bible describes matter as having weight which would not be discovered by science for centuries.[35]

When you read the creation story in Genesis you will find the phrase *"after his kind"* no less than 10 times in the very first chapter of Genesis. This clearly indicates that different species do not evolve but were separated genetically from the time of creation. Darwin used the example of finches as a way to demonstrate how evolution works but in his example no finch evolved into anything other than a finch. It is important to understand that when Christians claim to not believe in evolution that we are not saying we do not believe in changes within a species or micro-evolution. Micro-evolution is scientifically proven & is no way unbiblical. Macro-evolution is not scientific & is unbiblical. There is not one shred of scientific evidence that points to one species evolving into another species. Fish do not evolve into birds, apes do not evolve into humans this is pure fantasy that is being taught as science today in schools. (1 Corinthians 15:39) *"All flesh is not the same flesh: but there is one kind of flesh of men, another flesh of beasts, another of fishes, & another of birds."* [35]

The truth there is no way to prove scientifically any questions about creation because science can only exist when someone is able to observe & record what takes place. No one is able to observe the creation of the universe. When you simply look at anything in nature it always without exception grows old & dies. There is absolutely no scientific evidence to support the idea that species evolve over time into something more complex. It is quite apparent that it is the modern scientist who are disregarding the basic laws of science. While those who regard the Bible as true seem to accept the laws of science. [35]

Entropy vs. Evolution: Mutations are perfect examples of entropy. Mutations within a population will inevitably result in a decrease of organization. If mutations become wide-spread the population could die off yet evolution depends on mutations to not only preserve populations but advance them by natural selection to become better organized & more complex. However all scientific data suggests that mutations rarely, if ever improve populations but nearly always mutations harm & sometimes wipe out populations. Biblical evidence of the decay of cosmos is found in (Isaiah 51:6) *"Lift up your eyes to the heavens & look upon the earth beneath: for the heavens shall vanish away like smoke & the earth shall wax old like a garment." (Matt 24:35) "Heaven & earth shall pass away, but my words shall not pass away"*

Spontaneous Generation is the idea that living organisms could emerge from non-living materials is ancient. Greek philosopher believed in spontaneous generation as did the majority of other ancient philosopher. It was in the late 19th century that the Bible believing chemist Louis Pasteur demonstrated that spontaneous generation does not occur. Pasteur proved that life comes only from life & modern biology was born. Evolutionary biologist have diligently searched for other was to explain life but as of today have not been successful. In 1938 Russian chemist O.A. Oparin proposed the theory of Abiogenesis which stats that the first life arose from some primordial soup of complex chemicals through reactions with electrical discharges.

Later in 1953 Stanley Miller demonstrated how this could happen by devising an apparatus which repeatedly circulated a mixture of heated gases of water vapor, methane, ammonia, & hydrogen past an electric charge & each cycle produced a minute amount of liquid containing amino acids were caught in a trap. The scientific community embraced this as proof that life could be produced without life. Soon they were forced to acknowledge the truth that no trap like the one Miller used could have existed & even if it could exist & it did produce amino acids it would still fall short of proving that life could have ever been produced as amino acids are far less complex than the simplest protein molecule.

The origin of the genetic code is the most baffling aspect of the origins of life. The genetic code is far too complex to have originated naturally by chance. There are approximately 10 to the 20th power number of genetic codes possible & evolutionist simply accept that the exact genetic code just happened by chance...this is an enormous leap of faith. Think of it this way, for over 75 years the brightest scientist in the world have spent countless hours trying to produce life but have yet to come close, but they all accept it could have just happened by chance. *"The notion that the operating program of a living cell could be arrived at by chance in a primordial organic soup is nonsense of the highest order."* Sir Fred Doyle.[35]

*"God said let the earth bring forth the living creature **after his kind,** cattle & creeping thing, & beast of the earth **after his kind:** & it was so. & God made the beast of the earth **after his kind,** & cattle **after their kind, &** everything that creepeth upon the earth **after his kind.** & God saw that it was good.* (Gen 1:24-25). 5 times in 2 verses the Bible uses the phrase *"After his kind"* God created many kinds of animals which were designed to reproduce only within its kind. The variety of kinds of life on earth were created by God & did not evolve. Evolution certainly takes place within a kind but no kind of animal has ever evolved into another kind of animal. Evolutionist are puzzled as to how species originated. No new species has ever been observed evolving from another species. Modern paleontologists conclude that species seem to appear suddenly with no transitions.

Paleontologist George Gaylord Simpson, Curator of the Museum of Comparative Zoology at Harvard University from 1959 to 1970n said *"The earliest and most primitive members of every order already have the basic ordinal characters, and in no case is an approximately continuous series from one to another known. In most cases the break is so sharp and the gap so large that the origin of the order is speculative and much disputed"* This comes from a leading evolutionist...[36]

Every instance that evolutionist point to as proof of evolution it is nothing more than variation within a species. When the environment changes each species has the ability to adapt in order to survive. This has been observed in moths, fruit flies, & finches. This adaptation is amazing but it is not evolution of one species into another species.

The fossil record is the best evidence for evolution as it supposedly documents the evolutionary changes throughout history. The embarrassing truth for evolutionist is that there is not 1 single transitional evolutionary sequence found anywhere in the world. Both mammals & birds are assumed to have evolved from reptiles, the archaeopteryx is supposed to be the classic example of a transitional form, yet all of its features are fully developed & functional. Add to this that birds have been proven to exist earlier than the archaeopteryx and your back to square one. The evolutionary trees which are in our kids textbooks are missing data. In fact only the very tips of these evolutionary trees have been found. The clear evidence shows that no species arose gradually instead they all seem to appear together, all at once, fully developed. In fact there is a gradual admission among today's leading scientist that evidence points away from evolution. Dr. Duane Gish recently published "Evolution-The Fossils say NO." Now scientist are scrambling to find another theory to support before they are forced to accept that the Bibles account of creation & world-wide flood are the most scientifically reasonable theories.[37]

How did humans originate?

The third and most amazing act of creation in my opinion is the creation of man. The Bible describes man's creation this way (Gen 1:26) *"And God said, let us make man in our image, after our likeness: & let them have dominion over the fish of the sea, and over the fowl of the air, and over the cattle, and over all the earth"* The Bible make a clear distinction between man & animal. God created man in His image & likeness. Man has the ability to create, just as God creates. Man creates buildings, books, art, & music unlike other animals who do not have the capacity to create. No ape ever composed a song, wrote a novel, or built a house. The Bible's account of the creation of man is completely aligned with known science. Evolution teaches that man is simply a link in an evolutionary chain. Somewhere 10's of 1000's of years ago the first ape stood upright & walked... Evolutionist claim to have many examples of links between ape & man but so far none has been scientifically proven.[38]

  Biblical anthropology: According to the Bible man stands alone with respect to creation as man is said to have been created in the image of God. To the evolutionist man is merely one step higher on the evolutionary chain than the chimpanzee. Even though the scientific establishment is committed to the concept of human evolution, all the evidence seems to disagree. There is always great media attention given any apparent discovery of ape-men or missing links, invariably these discoveries are later found to be erroneous. Nebraska man turned out to be a peccary, Piltdown man was a hoax, and Java man was a composite of a man & a Gibbon.

The evidence clearly shows that human skulls have evolved over time. Human craniums are 1500 cubic centimeters today, but were only 1100 cubic centimeters 1000 years ago. The normal range of human craniums over the years is 800 cubic centimeters to nearly 2000 cubic centimeters. These measurements are very close to those of apes over the years. This makes it easy to take the skulls of apes & set them in line next to human skulls & say look evolution! This may be a clever way to suggest evolution from ape to man but it is not science.[38]

The life sciences: Over the past 120 years the life sciences have been skewed by the adherence to the philosophy of organic evolution. If modern scientist were willing to simply use the most basic laws of thermodynamics to determine how life began they would quickly dismiss evolution as a viable answer to how life began. Biologist who stubbornly refuse to accept the possibility that life came from a creator will never come to correct conclusions. The Bible clearly teaches that God created man from the dust of the earth. In fact everything God created came from the dust of the earth. This fits with scientific fact that all matter comes from the periodic table. This is amazing when you consider how vast & how diverse things are, yet they all are made up of the same elements. This certainly fits the Biblical account of God using the dust of the ground. In Genesis 2:7 the Bible says *"The Lord formed man of the dust of the ground, & breathed into his nostrils the breath of life; & man became a living soul."*

God used the breath of life to create life. This indicates that it may not be possible to understand life in terms of chemistry & physics. If life were simply a matter of chemistry & physics then I'm certain the most brilliant scientist of the last century would have made far greater strides in demonstrating how life came about than they have. If life only comes from God as the Bible teaches then the most brilliant scientist on earth will never come close to producing life from nothing.[39]

The problem is that modern psychologists & sociologists base much of their scientific data on the erroneous belief that there is an evolutionary community between man & other animals. While experiments on animals often do yield valuable information they do not give reliable insight to human behavior. There is no question that humans share many qualities of animals but there is no doubt that humans are much more complex. Humans create while animals do not, humans worship while animals do not, and humans speak in languages while animals do not. Despite numerous efforts to teach chimps to talk there is absolutely an unbridgeable gap between human language & the chattering's of animals. While animals may love...do they hate? Humans hate. It is a mistake for behavioral & social sciences to study animals in order to better understand human behavior.[39]

There has been a very fascinating development in the discovery of the pigmy chimpanzee also known as the Bonobo. The Bonobo are chimps that walk upright for long stretches at a time & they are understood to be the closest link between man & ape. This reveals one of the most dangerous attitudes that are born out evolution, which is the myth that certain apes are close to humans & certain humans are close to apes. The idea that certain races are more evolved than others is dangerous. It causes one race to justify subjugating other lesser races.

Charles Darwin's attitude toward the natives of Tierra del Fuego is indicative of this attitude. Darwin described the natives of Tierra del Fuego as much beast as man. They were mistaken as primitive cannibals who had not evolved as much as the white man. However, the British Catholic scholar Paul Kildare points out that the Tierra del Fuego natives were not cannibals at all, in fact Kildare reported that they had their own highly developed written language, they had high morals, & in fact considered Darwin & his crew to be morally inferior to themselves. Missionaries have found the same characteristics to be true everywhere. On every remote island, or in the deepest jungles there are people who were once believed to be primitive cannibals are instead very advanced, most have a written language, all have a sophisticated spoken language. They all worship some God or Gods, they have highly developed social structure. The fact is that when given the opportunity, they have the ability to succeed in higher education. To the extent that they now seem to fall short of modern civilization it seems to point to a fall from modern civilization rather than a rise from apes.[40]

There are those who see no reason for Christians to stand against evolution & they simply say that God used evolution to form man. This may be true but why would God choose to use evolution to create everything? I agree with Jonathan Sarfati who said *"A God who created by evolution is the same as no God at all" "Evolution is a philosophy trying to explain everything without God."* [41]

To me there is an enormous difference in teaching that man was formed By a God in the very image of a God who loves you, and in teaching that you are simply a link in an evolutionary chain & have no greater value than a monkey. We have taught our children that they come from monkeys & yet are appalled when our kids behave like monkeys. One of the troubling results of teaching evolution is the devaluing of human life. If evolution is true than why should it matter if Hitler kills millions of Jews, or that whites choose to enslave blacks, or that millions die of aids each year or that strait people bully & oppress gay people...after all its simple natural selection, only the strong survive right? If however we are created in the image of a loving God who cares deeply for each person, so much so that the Bible says that God knows the number of each hair of our heads. If this is true then every human life has great value making the slaughter of millions of Jews horrendous, the enslaving of others based on skin color unthinkable, the great loss of life due to aids is tragic, & oppressing those with different views is unacceptable. Paul warns us in (Romans 1:25) *"Man changed the truth of God into a lie & worshiped & served the creature more than the creator."* It should come as no surprise that modern science is no different that ancient religions that believed man somehow was formed out of water with no need of God.[42]

It troubles me at the number of Christians who choose to accept evolution as true & compatible with the Bible. Why believe a loving God would use the most wasteful, inefficient, cruel process ever designed to create the universe. Theologically, evolution is directly opposed to Biblical teachings. If God uses evolution to create the universe then you are saying that God is the author of pain & death. If Adam & Eve were the very first humans who would have evolved from apes who lived & died for millions of years, then death was already existing before Adam & Eve sinned. The Bible is clear that death is a result of man's sin. If evolution is true then the Bible is mistaken & God was allowing his perfect creation to die. Also understand if God, not man's sin, is responsible for death then how would Jesus taking on man's sin do anything to overcome death? [43]

Where did the world's thousands of languages come from?
Babel & the world population: Biblical demography & linguistics.
Families, nations, & races of mankind are not to be analyzed in
an evolutionary context. Humans are not like a hive of bees, or
herd of antelope. Demographics say that population is
perpetually increasing more rapidly in recent years. The world's
population is a little over 8 billion & if you make the assumption
that the average family had 2.5 children then it seems to point
to man beginning about 4500 years ago which fits the Biblical
chronology nicely as the flood is believed to have occurred 4500
years ago. However if you take the evolutionists assumption
that man has walked the earth for possibly 100,000 years then
the world's population should be far greater than 8 billion.[43]

We need to consider the remarkable phenomenon of the
various human languages, evolutionary theorists are incapable
of presenting a plausible model. How did man develop
language? If man developed language then why are there so
many totally different languages? These questions confound
evolutionist. One would assume that if human language evolved
that the more primitive tribes would naturally have a simple
language while civilized man would have a more complex
language. The truth is the most primitive tribes in the world
speak very complex languages. There is not the slightest
evidence, modern or ancient, of the evolution of language. The
oldest known languages that can be reasonably reconstructed
are just as complex & sophisticated as any modern language.
There are over 6000 languages now being spoken in the world &
all of them are equally complex.[43]

The Bible is Scientifically Reliable.

The confusion of tongues: As far as the great proliferation of different languages among men is concerned the Biblical account is the only satisfactory explanation. If all men came from one ancestral population they must have originally spoken the same language. Evolutionist have a problem understanding how so many different languages evolved. If anthropologists insist on an evolutionary explanation for the different languages, then they must postulate extremely long periods of isolation & inbreeding for the different tribes. It is natural to assume that some races evolved more than others. This natural association of racism with evolutionary philosophy is quite significant & is the basis of a wide range of racist political & religious philosophies that have wrought untold harm & misery over the years. The Bible teaches there is only one race of men...the human race.[43]

The Source of the different languages cannot be explained in terms of evolution. There are simply too many diverse languages to be explained in any naturalistic framework. Only the Bible provides an adequate explanation *"The whole earth was of one language, & one speech...The Lord did there confound the language of all the earth; & from thence did the Lord scatter them abroad upon the face of all the earth."*(Gen 11:1&9) The real divisions among men are not racial, or physical, or geographic, they are linguistic. When men could not understand one another they were forced to disperse. It is interesting to note there are other civilizations with stories of a time when everyone spoke the same language until the god's confused the languages. When you add to this the fact that God implanted in the 1st man & woman genetic information from which a wide variety of characteristics which could vary rapidly depending on the environment. Such rapid variation is not evolution but is simply a recombination of genetic factors already present. The small population of each family separated by language would have caused the distinctive characteristics that we see today in the different races. If one is committed to an evolutionary interpretation of the origin of races, it is necessary to assume a long evolutionary history of racial segregation, mutations, & natural selection to develop each distinctive set of racial characteristics. Hitler was so enamored with the evolutionary theory that he was willing to commit the lives of the German people to the struggle for racial supremacy. Hitler's campaign to destroy the Jews was merely good science, applied Darwinism.[43]

God & the Nations: Biblical ethnology, Ethnology is very broadly defined as the study of the origin & development of the various nations, peoples, & languages of the World. Because of evolutionary bias in the social sciences, Biblical revelation has not been taken seriously. The table of nations in Genesis 10 gives the most important information on the origin of nations. According to the Bible, civilization began in the Middle East, specifically in the general vicinity of Mt. Ararat, in modern day Turkey. The post-Babel dispersion of the nations can be traced to Noah's descendants, Japheth, Shem, & Ham.[43]

The Japhetic nations have been identified as Javen (Greece), Magog, Mesheck, & Tubal (Russia), Gomer & Ashkenaz (Germany), Madai (Medes), and Togarmah (Armenia). Most of these people migrated into Europe & became what is known today as the Caucasian races. Who later migrated to America & Australia. The Shemites listed have been identified as Eber, (Hebrews), Elam, (Persians), Aram (Syrians), Asshur, (Assyria), they stayed near the Mediterranean & Middle East.

The Bible is Scientifically Reliable.

The Hamites are identified: Mizraim (Egypt), Cush (Ethiopia), Put (Lybia), Khetae (China), these families migrated into Asia & Africa.

Wherever one finds firm evidence of human societies, he finds evidence of a high order of intelligence & technology very early in the history of that site. According to evolution man began to hunt & gather & the Stone Age followed, man learned how to use tools, then the Bronze Age followed, man developed metal then the Iron Age followed. The fact is that there are primitive cultures who are hunters & gatherers today. There were advanced cultures over 3000 years ago in Egypt & in South America with the Mayan's. It seems that the supposed evolutionary divisions are meaningless. One could teach a stone aged savage into a 21st century doctorate in a matter of years, Evolutionary stages are not needed to properly describe how civilization grew.[43]

Archeologist & Anthropologist have attempted to divide early human history into periods. The Paleolithic or Old Stone Age which is where the 1st apes began to walk upright & man had evolved & had begun to hunt & gather. Then there is the Mesolithic or Middle Stone Age which is where man began to cultivate crops & settle together. Then there is the Neolithic or New Stone Age which is where man began villages & economy began. Once man discovered how to use metals the Bronze Age began & cities began to spring up. The origin of 5 accoutrements of civilization are 1. Pottery 2. Agriculture 3. Animal Husbandry 4. Metallurgy 5. Cities.

The Bible is Scientifically Reliable.

The interesting thing is that all of these things seem to have appeared at the same time in the Middle East as the Bible records. Ceramics were being fired as early as 9000 B.C. (according to evolutionist) The Bible records that Abel, the son of Adam kept sheep. It is apparent that man was civilized from day 1.

The Biblical account of early human history is supported by archeology. After the flood God commanded man to go spread out all over the world. Man instead gathered together & became extremely advanced as a society. They were so advanced that they believed they could reach the status of God's themselves. This is when God confused their languages & men were scattered all over the world. This is where archeologists are beginning to reconstruct their migrations & settlements. As populations grew, so did the competition for the most desirable places. So the strongest, most advanced families & tribes acquired & developed the best locations. Wars were fought to defend or to gain territory, those who were defeated were forced to migrate farther away & settle less hospitable lands.

When the populations began to grow in these areas competition for the prime land began all over & the scenario repeated over & over. In this scenario you would expect for small groups of defeated families & tribes would be forced to isolated areas where there would be more inbreeding, inadequate diets, causing general degeneracy & many would simply die out while those able to survive would live primitive lives far from the civilized world. All real data seems to describe the Bibles account of ancient history.

It seems as though man has not slowly evolved from animals but that man has always been man, highly intelligent, & skillful, capable of rapidly developing viable & complex civilizations wherever he has gone.[43]

The Biblical account of a world-wide flood is scientifically reliable.

One of the most ridiculed stories in the Bible is the story of the flood. Ironically every civilization in the world has a story of a world-wide flood. Most scientist accept uniformitarianism which stats that the present processes we see today operated the exact same way throughout all of time. Amazingly the Bible predicted that man would one day accept this idea.

(2 Peter 3:3-4) *"There shall come in the last days scoffers, walking after their own lusts saying where is the promise of his coming? For since the fathers fell asleep, all things continue as they were from the beginning."*

(Psalm 104:6) *"Thou coverest it with the deep as with a garment: the waters stood above the mountains."*

In the creation story the Bible seems to refer to a canopy of water above the earth, as well as a great amount of water below the earth. (Gen 1:7) *"And God made the firmament, and divided the waters which were under the firmament from the waters which were above the firmament."* (Gen 7:11) *" ...All the fountains of the great deep broken up, & the windows of heaven were opened."* Critics of a world-wide flood say that there is not enough water in 40 days & nights of rain to flood the entire earth. They are right, the Bible is clear that not only did water fall from the heavens for 40 days & nights it also rose from below the earth.

Scientist now know that all 7 continents were all connected forming one large landmass known as Pangaea. The Bible seems to allude to Pangaea here (Gen 1:9) *"Let the waters under the heaven be gathered together unto one place, and let the dry land appear: and it was so."* When you read this & then read how the Bible describes the great deep breaking up it seems to be suggesting that there was a great eruption of water from below the earth which actually broke up the earth. This sounds like Pangaea being torn apart suddenly as great amounts of water come up from within the earth which would have caused a great shift in the tectonic plates causing the continents to divide as well as flooding the earth with water.[43]

Dr. Joseph Dillow published the most detailed study of this presumed water canopy in his book *"The Waters Above"*. This canopy provides an excellent explanation of a wide range of scientific as well as Biblical truths. When the great upheaval of water came bursting through the earth it must have either been caused by or resulted in volcanoes erupting releasing magma which would have formed Islands as the earthquakes caused the tectonic plates to slide apart causing Pangaea to separate into the 7 continents we see today. All of this volcanic ash in the air would have caused the water canopy above the earth to condense and fall which would explain the 40 days & nights of heavy rain. With the vapor canopy removed it caused storm systems, heavy winds, & of course rainbows for the first time.

This also started the different seasons as well as reduced the lifespan of all living things on earth. The water levels were at their highest right after the world-wide flood as water covered the entire earth. This explains why we see sea shells on every inch of the earth today. The water continues to recede to this day. This is why the world's rivers flow at the bottom of great valleys & canyons. The flood waters cut the canyons & valleys and the receding waters simply run through the earth's lowest points. This is far more scientific than suggesting that the rivers actually carved the canyons over millions of years. This would also explain why today's deserts were once well watered & were homes of some great cities but today are home only to nomads.[44]

Dillow explains how a vapor canopy could have existed & how it would have lengthened the lives of not only men but of every creature on the earth. He suggests that this is where dinosaurs came from. Reptiles which lived 10 times longer than they do today would have grown to enormous sizes which may explain dinosaurs & why they do not live today. Could it be that they are simply reptiles who no longer live long enough to grow so large?[44]

The ark is the only ship whose dimensions are recorded in the Bible. The ark was essentially a huge box built for stability not mobility. The ark was taller than a 3 story building & 1 ½ times as long as a football field making it approximately 140,000 cubic feet. This is large enough to hold 522 standard railroad car. A standard railroad car can hold 240 sheep. A sheep is slightly larger than the average size of all animals. This means the ark could hold 125,000 sheep comfortably. When you take in account that there are only 18,000 known species of land animals on earth today then you can see that the ark certainly could have held 2 of every land animal on earth.[44]

Overflowed with water: Geology is the study of the earth & is compatible with the Bible. However today there is a branch of geology that is known as historic geology. An interesting fact about historical geologist is they are not historians & are very poor geologist. They profess to be able to decipher the supposed long evolutionary history of the earth by studying the earth's sedimentary crust & the fossils contained in them. Unlike real geology which applies the laws of nature, historic geology must leave the realm of science & enter into philosophy or even a sort of religion whose basic doctrine is uniformitarianism. Darwin acknowledged that his theory of evolution by natural selection depended on long ages & slow changes provided by uniformity.[45]

James Hutton, a Scottish geologist, published *"The Theory of Earth."* In 1785. Hutton maintained that the present is the key to the past, & that given enough time, processes observed today could account for all the geologic features of the earth. This became known as the doctrine of uniformitarianism. The scientific community bought it, hook, line, & sinker! This doctrine is today universally accepted by most scientist. By assuming that all the earth's processes remain constant throughout time it allows for radioactive decay, continental erosion, the earth's climate, & many other processes to have extremely long chronological values, which are far greater than the Bible records. This has caused many Christians to accept the possibility that the flood of the Bible was localized & not world-wide.

The Bible is very clear the flood was a world-wide catastrophe. (Gen 7:19) *"The waters prevailed exceedingly upon the earth; & all the high hills that were under the whole heaven were covered."* This is certainly not describing some localized flood as many try to believe. Also consider God's promise (Gen.9:11) *"...I will establish my covenant with you...neither shall there anymore be a flood to destroy the earth."* If the Bible is referring to a local flood then God is a liar. There are localized floods which occur all over the world every year. Of course God is no liar & his promise to never destroy the world by flood is still true.[45]

 What if things do change? What if processes that we see today did not always work as they do now? Robert Dott, a professor at the Univ. of Wisconsin, stresses that the geological record as preserved in sedimentary rocks is a record of catastrophes instead of slow uniformity. Eposodicity is the rule not the exception. If you accept a world-wide flood then you would expect to find some clues like ... evidence of sea life all over the world, the tallest mountains, driest deserts, deepest valleys. Evidence of large numbers of animals buried quickly in water & mud. Piles of sodium deposits all around the world. Deep canyons cut by rushing water as it rose quickly. If there was a world-wide flood then you would find stories from all over the world describing it, not just the Bible. We do find all of these today. In fact we find that the fossils are buried in order of super-position. Simpler life forms unable to swim or fly would be trapped earlier & buried deeper & the animals which could swim or fly would drown later & be buried shallower.[45]

You would of course expect to find a few exceptions. You would also expect to find areas of many fossils with large areas with absolutely no fossils, as the waters would carry fossils & deposit them together. Have you noticed when flooded creek waters recedes it leaves areas of brush, trash, & muck behind. It does not scatter debris equally. This evidence fits the Biblical flood much better than uniformity. If there were no world-wide flood & everything occurred uniformly over millions of years then you would not expect to find evidence of sea life on top of the highest mountains or in the driest deserts, you would not expect to only find fossils in small pockets that are packed full of fossils while large areas of land have no fossils.

Most troubling of all is you would not expect to find complex modern animal fossils alongside primitive simple fossils as is found all over the world. If the geologic column is real, & if evolution is true, then why do we find fossils from one evolutionary age mixed in with fossils from other evolutionary ages? Better yet how it that the fossil of one dinosaur or tree often crosses layers of sediment that are supposedly hundreds of years apart?[45]

Modern day hydraulic engineers & Geo hydrologists are providing valuable insight to the real nature of the geologic column which are fully consistent with the Biblical account of the world-wide flood, & inconsistent with uniformity. Was what we find in the geologic column formed slowly over millions of years or was it formed rapidly during a great catastrophe such as a world-wide flood? It is well observed & recorded scientifically as to how rapid the decay process is. It is unreasonable to assume that the bodies of 10's of 1000's of animals remained intact long enough to be fossilized. In fact we have found fossils of one animal eating another. How did this happen over time? Then there are the embarrassing examples of one fossil of a tree or dinosaur that covers several layers of sediment which supposedly covers 100's of years. Then there is the presence of fossils from one evolutionary age found along fossils from a completely different evolutionary age.

Did you realize that most early geologist & scientist in general accepted the world-wide flood as the Bible describes as being responsible for the earth's sedimentary rocks & great bed of fossils? Men like Nicolaus Steno, the father of stratigraphy. John

Woodward, founder of the paleontological museum at Cambridge. Not to mention the father of modern science itself Sir Isaac Newton. The Biblical flood provides a far more effective model for correlating all the real data of geology than doe's historic geology. The geologic column occurs only in textbooks, it does not exist anywhere else in the world.[45]

Biblical miracles, dragons, & unicorns as they relate to science.

 The Bible mentions dragons, unicorns, behemoths, & leviathans which most liberal commentaries interpret as legendary animals. However it seems reasonable to me that these all describe dinosaurs. The word dinosaur is a relatively new word which would not have been a part of the language during the time the text was written or translated. Add to this the fact that these words, especially dragon which is used in many different civilizations to describe dinosaur like creatures. The word dragon is used 25 times in the Old Testament & in a few of these references there are specific descriptions of dragons which seem to describe what we would call dinosaurs. (Micah 1:8) *"...I will make a wailing like the dragons, & mourning as the owls."* This illustrates that the dragon's referred to here is just as literal as the owl & that humans heard the dragon just as humans heard owls, meaning that men dwelled with the dinosaurs just as the fossils indicate.

 (Jeremiah 14:6) *"The wild asses did stand in the high places, they snuffed up the wind like dragons"* This verse compares donkeys who snort & are literal to dragons who snort & must have been just as observable as donkeys as Jeremiah compares the snorts of wild donkeys to the snorts of dragons. (Duet 32:33) *"There wine is the poison of dragons, & the cruel venom of asps."* Moses was describing those who foolishly rebel

93

against God here in this chapter. He had compared them to bitter grapes, venom of snakes, & here poison of dragons. Once again dragons must have been literal & as observable as grapes & snakes. Some of them must have been full of poison as described here by Moses.

The problem with the Bible describing dragons with such detail in the same way it describes snakes, donkeys, & grapes is that dinosaurs according to evolution died out 70 million years ago & did not exist with humans. So the dragons described in the Bible & were obviously observed must not be dinosaurs but possibly reptiles like the Komodo dragon. However maybe dragons are dinosaurs & maybe they existed alongside humans. After all every civilization has legends of men hunting or running from dragons or dinosaurs. Notice the descriptions of the behemoth & leviathan described in the book of Job.

(Job: 40:15-18) *"Behold now behemoth which I made with thee; he eateth grass as an ox. Lo now, his strength is in his loins, & his force is in the naval of his belly. He moveth his tail like a cedar; the sinews of his stones are wrapped together. His bones are as strong pieces of brass; his bones are like bars of iron."* Listen to this description of the leviathan in this summary of Job: 41. *" Canst thou draw out leviathan with an hook?...none is so fierce that dare stir him up...his teeth are terrible round about, his scales are his pride..., out his his mouth go burning lamps, & sparks of fire leap out. Out of his nostrils goeth smoke, as out of a seething pot or caldron, His breadth kindleth coals, & a flame goeth out of his mouth...The arrow cannot make him flee; sling stones are turned with him into stubble...upon the earth there is not his like."*

Most any educated person would no doubt scoff at the idea of a fire breathing dragon. However the Bible seems to be describing a fire breathing dragon. Combine this with the fact that most civilizations have legions of fire breathing dragons. I know this sounds unreasonable but this is not unheard of. Fire flies produce glowing light from its tail, electric eels produce electricity, & then there is the little known bombardier beetle which produces an explosive chemical reaction which appears as though it shoots fire. So it is not unrealistic to assume that some dinosaurs actually breathed fire. It is definitely not unbiblical.[46]

Unicorns are mentioned 9 times in the Old Testament. When you take all 9 references to unicorns you get this description of the unicorn. They were powerful animals with great strength, they obviously had one single horn, & they came out from Egypt. Biblical commentators all have different opinions of what these unicorns were. Some say they were rhino like animals, others compare them with bulls, while others say they resemble the horse with one horn which fits the legendary image of the unicorn. The fact is that the Bible claims that an animal known as a unicorn really existed, therefore they certainly must have existed. Scientifically speaking it is not unreasonable to assume the unicorn could have existed & became extinct.[47]

The Bible reveals many scientific truths far earlier than science discovered them.

The Bible is not a scientific text book, it is however scientifically reliable. When the Bible deals with a scientific principle, or some particular item of scientific data, it will inevitably be found to be true in its scientific insights. As a matter of fact, the Bible often anticipates scientific discoveries. Many critics of the Bible assume that the Bible falsely describes the earth as flat. They often claim that Christians were the ones who believed that the world was flat. Certainly many did but they did so not because the Bible taught that the world was flat but because the scientific world believed that the world was flat. The Bible is accurate in its description of the earth. (Isaiah 40:22) *"It is he that sitteth upon the circle of the earth...& stretcheth out the heavens as a curtain & spread them out as a tent."* [47]

Hydrology is the science of water. The Bible gives an amazingly accurate description of the hydrologic cycle, which was recently discovered by modern scientist. (Ecc 1:7) *"All the rivers run into the sea, yet the sea is not full, unto the place from whence the rivers came tither they return again."* (Isaiah 55:10) *"For as the rain cometh down & the snow from heaven & returneth not tither, but watereth the earth, & maketh it bring forth & bud, that it may give seed to the sower, and bread to the eater."* The Bible explains how the rains on land originate in the evaporated water from the ocean. The Bible also suggests that air has weight 1000's of years before science discovered atmospheric pressure.

 (Job 28:25) *"To make the weight for the winds; & he weigheth the waters by measure."* The Bible also describes mountains & channels within the ocean. (Psalm 18:15) *"Then the channels of waters were seen & the foundations of the world were discovered"* (Psalm 8:8) *"The fowl of the air, & fish of the sea, & whatsoever passeth through the paths of the sea."* Matthew Maurey is known as the father of oceanography & as a Bible believing Christian he used these Biblical passages which referred to the seas having paths to discover the great oceanic circulations. Maurey became known as the path finder of the seas.[47]

The fact that blood sustains life is a relatively modern concept. It was in 1616 that William Harvey discovered the circulation of blood in the body. Blood is vital to life, it carries nourishment to every cell, transmits hormones, maintains the body's temp, & removes the waste of the body's cells. The Bible teaches that blood sustains life. (Lev.17:11) *"The life of the flesh is in the blood."* Blood also has a vital spiritual importance in the Bible. Since physical life is maintained by blood it is reasonable to say that spiritual life is also maintained by blood. This is why Abel's sacrifice of lambs was accepted by God while Cain's sacrifice of plants was not accepted by God. Blood represents life, & the penalty of sin is death, therefore blood was needed to atone for man's sin. Plants represent man's work & there is no work of man that can pay for man's sin. Blood is needed for life, physical & spiritual.[47]

Jacob demonstrated principles of modern genetics in Genesis 31. Jacob spent decades raising livestock & had learned many principles of genetics. He used this knowledge to trick Laban. Jacob understood that even in a flock of solid colored goats there would be some that were heterozygous that is they had within their genetic endowment the ability to produce a small number of speckled goats. Using this knowledge & by sound principles of selective breeding Jacob was able to produce a flock of goats whose dominate coloration was spotted & speckled instead of solid coloring. In doing this Jacob was able to take the larger number of spotted goats, leaving Laban with only a few solid colored goats. This account is in perfect harmony with the known principles of modern genetics.[47]

The Trinity is very scientific. The God of the Bible is a triune God. That is there is only one God who is really 3 separate entities. God the Father, God the Son, & God the Holy Spirit.

The Bible is Scientifically Reliable.

The doctrine of the trinity & that God became flesh are both unique & fundamental doctrines of Christianity. This doctrine offends many & defies logic to others. It is interesting to note that the idea of a trinity is compatible with the very nature of the cosmos. For over 1000 years now science has understood that the universe consist of 3 things space, matter, & time. All of the physical processes of matter in the universe cannot exist without space & cannot be realized without time. Therefore the universe is a trinity. It is one universe which has three distinct forms that are interdependent upon one another. It is not that the universe is a triad of three distinct entities when added together form the whole. It is rather that each is itself wholly distinct from the other two, yet could never exist without the other two.

If you remove one part of the universe then the universe would no longer exist. The universe is a trinity which is remarkably analogous to the nature of its creator.[48]

Now consider that space is itself a trinity of 3 dimensions. There is length, width, & height. Each is infinite in its extent & occupies the whole of space. Yet no one dimension can exist alone. A simple line must have both length & width to be represented in 2 dimensions, on paper, yet even a line needs 3 dimensions to exist in reality. Space in its fullness is measured in terms of its volume which is obtained by multiplying instead of adding. Therefore the mathematics of a trinity is not 1+1+1=3 it is rather 1x1x1=1 which is profoundly true. God existing as a trinity can be explained mathematically with perfect sense, which is that God is made up of father x son x spirit = God.[48]

What about time? Time is also a trinity. Time consists of past, present, & future. Each is distinct yet completely dependent of the other two. One part of time could not exist without the other two. There could be no present unless there is a past preceding it nor could there be any future unless there is a present. Matter, in its broadest sense, is also a trinity of sorts. Matter must have a cause which starts an event which leads to a consequence which produces energy. This is easier to understand mathematically, Cause x event (effect) x energy (work) = Matter. So in a remarkable way the universe is a trinity of trinities created by a triune God. Imagine that the God of the Bible makes perfect sense it is not only reasonable but amazingly probable. There is profound scientific truth in the triune nature of God.[48]

There is also a profound scientific truth in the dual nature of Jesus Christ who the Bible says was both God & Man. For centuries theologians have debated this difficult concept. Some say Jesus must have been 50% God & 50% Man, but the Bible is perfectly clear that Jesus was 100% God while being 100% Man. At face value this seems impossible but recent scientific discoveries have been made concerning the dual nature of light. Physical light has two contradictory yet somehow harmonious natures. Light can manifest itself through waves of motion or it can be manifested through a stream of particles.

 This is one of the great paradoxes of science that has become known as the principle of indeterminacy. It has also led to the principle of complementarity which may have been formalized in modern physics, but it was anticipated in scripture long before the development of modern physics. This may seem like a bit of a stretch comparing Jesus with light, but the Bible in fact teaches that both God & Jesus are in fact best described as light. (1 John 1:5) *"God is light, in him is no darkness at all."* Jesus describes himself as light. (John 8:12) *"Jesus said, I am the light of the world: he that followeth me shall not walk in darkness at all"* Also consider that the very first thing God created was light. (Gen 1:3) *"God said, let there be light & there was light."* The dual nature of Christ & the triune God maybe difficult to understand but they are in no way unscientific.[49]

When you examine the Bible it aligns with the laws of science just as you would expect from a book given to us by the very creator of the universe. There is no need to be intimidated with the elitism of today's modern scientist who grasp onto unscientific theories and accept them as fact while sneering at those who take God at His Word.

I would challenge you to open your mind and objectively compare the Bible with today's modern scientific theories and ask yourself which is more plausible?

The Bible is prophetically accurate

"Show the things that are come here after, that we may know that ye are gods." (Isaiah 41:23)

The Bible's prophetic accuracy is what separates it from every other book ever written. As far as religious books go the Bible is the only one to include any prophecy at all. This is important in that if the Bible is in fact the word of God and it makes claims concerning the future and they do not occur then one would question the validity of the entire book. The Bible includes over 2000 prophecies which have already been fulfilled! This is overwhelming evidence supporting the fact that the Bible stands alone as God's word.

In this chapter I would like to show you a few of the more remarkable fulfilled prophecies in the Bible, starting with the fall of 4 ancient cities. Then we will look at the most remarkable prophecy concerning Jerusalem's Eastern gate. Next we will look at the prophecies Jesus fulfilled at his birth. We will also look at 2 amazing Old Testament chapters Isaiah 53 which describes Jesus life, and Psalm 22 which describe Jesus crucifixion. Finally, I would like to briefly look at the rapture of the church.

The Bibles prediction of the fall of the 4 ancient cities of Nineveh, Tyre, Babylon, and Samaria. When you consider that the Bible has even one fulfilled prophecy it is remarkable, but when you realize there are over 2000 fulfilled prophecies in scripture, it boggles the mind. Many critics like to say that the Bibles prophecies are vague and can be explained away, I wonder if these critics have looked closely at the Bible's prediction of the fall of 4 ancient cities. They include very specific details that when added together are unexplainable. In Peter Stoner's book *Science Speaks* he uses the principle of probability to show just how amazing Biblical prophecies really are. Here is Stoner's principle of probability: if the chance of one thing happening is **A** & the chance of another independent thing happening is **B** then the chances of both things happening would be **A x B.**

Here is an example of how the principle of probability works, If the chance of someone being bald is 1:10 & the chances of someone being left handed is 1:10 then the chances someone being bald and left handed would be 1:100. Using Stoner's principle of probability it reveals the amazing accuracy of Biblical prophecies.[1]

We will first look at the Bible's prophecies concerning the fall of the ancient city of Nineveh. *"Out of the land went forth Asshur, and builded Nineveh..."* (Genesis 10:11). Nineveh is one of the earliest settlements in human history with its origins dating around 6000 B.C. It was the largest city on earth between 800 BC and its fall in 612 BC, with a population of nearly 200,000 people. It was home to a large library which included many writings of Assyrian philosophers which Plato would later study. There was a great wall surrounding the city nearly 8 miles in circumference & over 100 ft. tall. It had 15 gates & 120 towers that rose nearly 250 ft. The Tigris River ran under its great walls providing plenty of resources with which to survive any siege.[2]

In 654 BC God gives the prophet Nahum an amazing prophecy concerning the Assyrian capital of Nineveh. *"The burden of Nineveh. The book of the vision of Nahum."* (Nahum 1:1) There are 5 details included in Nahum's prophecy concerning the fall of Nineveh which all came true 42 years after Nahum predicted.

1. Nineveh would fall with an overrunning flood. *"But with an overrunning flood he will make an utter end of the place thereof, and darkness shall pursue his enemies"* (Nahum 1:8). Stoner places the odds of a city being flooded at 1:2

2. The Ninevites would be drunk during the invasion. *"For while they be folden together as thorns, and while they are drunken as drunkards, they shall be devoured as stubble fully dry."* (Nahum 1:10). Stoner places the odds of a city being invaded while it's army is drunk at 1:10

3. Nineveh would fall quickly with remarkable ease. *"All thy strongholds shall be like fig trees with the firstripe figs: if they be shaken, they shall even fall into the mouth of the eater."* (Nahum 3:12). Stoner's odds that a city would fall easy at 1:2.

4. Nineveh would be burned. (Nahum 3:13-15) *"The fire shall devour thy bars...there shall the fire devour thee..."* (Nahum 3:13-15). Stoner's odds of a city being burned is 1:2.

5. Nineveh would never recover. (Nahum 3:19) *"There is no healing of thy bruise, thy wound is grievous..."* (Nahum 3:19). Stoner places the odds that Nineveh would never recover at 1:20.

Using Stoner's principle of probability, the odds that all 5 of Nahum's prophecies concerning Nineveh would take place as predicted at 1:1600. So what happened?

In 612 BC the Babylonian leader Nabopolasser laid siege to Nineveh for 3 months they dammed the Tigris River and allowed nothing in or out of the city with no results. King Ashburbanal ordered a celebration of the indestructible city of Nineveh. While they drank it came a heavy rain which caused the Babylonian dam to break sending a flood of water rushing under the wall of Nineveh which quickly eroded the wall causing it to fall and allowed the Babylonian army to march in and burn the city while the Assyrian army watched in a drunken stupor. Nineveh lies in ruins to this day.[3]

The earliest known records of Tyre are found in the Bible as it mentions King Hiram of Tyre often trading with King David and Solomon for lumber to build the temple. *"And Hiram King of Tyre sent messengers to David, and cedar trees, and carpenters, and masons: and they built David an house."* (2 Samuel 5:11) *"Also cedar trees in abundance: for the Zidonians and they of Tyre brought much cedar wood to David."* (1 Chron. 22:4). We know that David ruled Israel around 1000 B.C. so the city of Tyre was obviously established before 1000 B.C. Most archeologist date Tyre back to 2750 B.C. and seem to agree that Tyre was at its peak between 1000 B.C. and 573 B.C when it was considered to be the largest port in the world, which boasted of having skyscrapers, city squares, & the largest navy in the world.[4]

The prophet Ezekiel was given a prophecy by God in 590 B.C. concerning the fall of this great port city of Tyre. **(Ezekiel 26:3-16)** In this passage Ezekiel makes 4 incredibly detailed predictions about Tyre.

1. Many nations would unite against the city of Tyre. *"Therefore thus saith the Lord God; behold, I am against thee, O Tyrus, and will cause many nations to come up against thee..."* (Ezekiel 26:3). Stoners odds 1:5

2. Tyre would be scraped flat like the top of a rock. *"And they shall destroy the walls of Tyrus, and break down*

her towers; I will also scrape her dust from her, and make her like the top of a rock." (Ezekiel 26:4). Now this is specific, anyone may predict the fallen walls & towers, but to predict that the city of tyre be scraped flat is quite specific. Stoner's odds 1:500

3. Nebuchadnezzar shall take the city of Tyre. *"Behold I will bring upon Tyrus Nebuchadrezzar King of Babylon, a king of kings, from the north, with horses, and with chariots, and with horsemen, and companies, and much people. He shall sley with the sword..."* (Ezekiel 26:7-8). Here, Ezekiel gets very specific in actually naming the exact King who would invade Tyre. Nebuchadnezzar had great power and desired to expand so this is not a great reach. Stoner's odds 1:3

4. Tyre's stones and timber will be thrown into the sea. *"And they shall make a spoil of thy riches, and make a prey of thy merchandise: and they shall break down thy walls, and destroy thy pleasant houses: and they shall lay thy stones and thy timber and thy dust in the midst of the water."* (Ezekiel 26:12). This prediction defies all logic as Ezekiel predicts that the valuable timber and stones be thrown in the sea instead of used for other purposes. Stoner's odds 1:10.

Stoner places the odds of all 4 of Ezekiel's very specific prophecies concerning Tyre coming to pass are 1:75,000.

In 573 B.C., 17 years after Ezekiel predicted that Tyre would fall, Nebuchadnezzar laid siege to Tyre for 13 years before finally taking the city of Tyre, only to find it empty as the people of Tyre had moved onto an island ½ mile off the coast, taking their riches with them. Frustrated, Nebuchadnezzar went back to

Babylon empty handed. Tyre would no longer be the largest port in the world but it did survive and was not at all leveled to the ground as Ezekiel had predicted.

It seemed as though Ezekiel got it only partially right and to this day critics point this fact out. However, in 332 B.C Alexander the great had heard of the great riches in Tyre so he enlisted help from competing ports and together they invaded and completely destroyed the city of Tyre in search of its great riches. When he discovered that the cities riches lie ½ mile off the coast he had the city leveled and all the timber, stones, and dust of the ground thrown into the sea in an attempt to build a causeway to the Island. This enormous endeavor took 7 months but eventually Alexander did reach the island and took the riches of Tyre. Tyre would never regain its status as a major port city but instead has become a sleepy little fishing village just as Ezekiel predicted. *"It shall be a place for the spreading of nets in the midst of the sea..."* (Ezekiel 26:5). [5]

Babylon is one of the oldest known civilizations in the world. The Bible credits Nimrod for establishing Babel. *"And Cush begat Nimrod: he began to be a mighty one in the earth...and the beginning of his kingdom was Babel...in the land of Shinar."* (Gen. 10:8-10). After the great flood all of humanity gathered in Babel, making it the greatest city in the world. The Bible describes the rise of Babel and the confusion of human language in Genesis 11. The ancient city of Babylon was the world's greatest city between 1790 B.C. until 1670 B.C. One of the world's most famous archeological finds is the Hammurabi Code which dates to 1772 B.C. There are several Biblical prophecies concerning Babylon, most of them deal with Babylon's invasion of Israel and the leading of the Jews into captivity for 70 years. I will focus on the prophecies concerning the fall of Babylon right now.[6]

Both Isaiah and Jeremiah make prophecies concerning Babylon's fall. Isaiah was written in 681 B.C. while Jeremiah was written in 626 B.C. They both predict Babylon would fall.

1. Babylon will fall. *"And Babylon, the glory of kingdoms, the beauty of the Chaldees Excellency, shall be as when God overthrew Sodom and Gomorrah."* (Isaiah 13:19). *"And the land shall tremble and sorrow, for every purpose of the Lord shall be performed against Babylon, to make the land of Babylon a desolation without an inhabitant."* (Jeremiah 51:29). Stoner's odds 1:2

2. Babylon shall never be inhabited again. *"It shall never be inhabited, neither shall it be dwelt in from generation to generation: neither shall the Arabian pitch tent there; neither shall the shepherds make their fold there."* (Isaiah 13:20). *"And Babylon shall become heaps...without an inhabitant."* (Jeremiah 51:37). Critics of Biblical prophecy often claim that the prophecies written concerning historical events must have been written after the events took place. This is the only logical explanation considering how detailed and accurate the prophecies are. This particular prophecy is confounding to the critics because even if you accept their own claims that much of these prophecies were written after Alexander the Great then it still boggles the mind that Babylon, to this day, has yet to be inhabited. Stoner's odds 1:100

3. No stone will be removed from Babylon. *"And they shall not take of thee a stone for a corner, nor a stone for*

foundations; but thou shalt be desolate forever."
(Jeremiah 51:26). Again this is extremely unlikely for no
stone to be taken from the ruins of Babylon & used for
construction. There are amazing pictures of the ruins of
Babylon taken by soldiers serving in Iraq. They picture a
heap of stones piled in the desert untouched for
thousands of years...remarkable. Stoner's odds 1:100

4. Here we have 2 seemingly conflicting prophecies.
    Babylon will become a desert. *" I will dry up her sea,
    and make her springs dry."*(Jeremiah 51:36). Stoner's
    odds 1:2. Babylon will be flooded. *"The sea is come
    upon Babylon: she is covered with the multitude of
    waves thereof."* (Jeremiah 51:42). Stoner's odds 1:2.
    Critics love to claim that the Bible includes so many
    prophetic statements that anyone can claim that a few
    come true. Here it seems the Bible will get one of these
    wrong will Babylon become a desert or will it be
    covered with waves?

*** There are 2 other prophecies mentioned in Isaiah do not
mention Babylon by name yet I have included them because
they are certainly implied. ***

5. Babylon will fall to Cyrus due to the fact the gates won't
    shut. *" Thus saith the Lord to his anointed, to Cyrus,
    whose right hand I have holden, to subdue nations
    before him; and I will loose the loins of kings, to open
    before him the 2 leaved gates; and the gates shall not
    be shut."* (Isaiah 45:1). This prophecy is full of very
    specific details, the name of the conqueror and the
    stroke of good fortune that allowed him to take
    Babylon. Stoner puts the odds conservatively at 1:500.

Stoner places the odds of these 5 prophecies concerning Babylon coming true at 1: 80,000. So what happened to Babylon? In 539 B.C. , 142 years after Isaiah's prophecy and 87 years after Jeremiah's prophecy, King Cyrus defeats the Babylonian army in the battle of Opis leaving only the city walls to defend the great city of Babylon. The walls were by all accounts impenetrable so Cyrus devised a way to go under the walls. The Euphrates River ran under 2 gates so Cyrus ordered his army to dig a canal to divert enough water from the Euphrates which allowed the army to simply march under the gates of Babylon. Once in the city Cyrus easily conquered the mighty city of Babylon.

Babylon would never be inhabited but there were a couple of times that powerful men did try to rebuild the ancient city. In 331 B.C. Alexander the Great planned on rebuilding Babylon but died unexpectedly at the age of 33. U.S. intelligence found plans that Saddam Hussein was attempting to bring tourist into Iraq by rebuilding the ancient city of Babylon, but the war with America obviously stalled any construction on the sight. Amazingly every prophecy concerning Babylon has come true, even the conflicting prophecies that Babylon would become a desert which is obviously true, and that Babylon would be flooded. The Euphrates River floods annually between March and May when melting snows in the Turkish highlands cause the Euphrates River to flood.

Today you can visit the ancient ruins of this once great city located in Iraq. There are some powerful images of the 1000's of stones scattered on the desert floor. No one lives here, not even shepherds, or nomads, in fact there are stories told by Iraq veterans that most people who live near these ruins will not dare step foot on the land because it is cursed.[7]

Samaria was the capital of the northern kingdom of Israel from 871 B.C. to 721 B.C. Samaria is first mentioned in *"And he bought the hill Samaria of Shemer for two talents of silver, and built on the hill, and called the name of the city which he built, after the name of Shemer, owner of the hill, Samaria."* (1 Kings 16:24). Omri was the 6th king of the northern kingdom who purchased a hill in 885 B.C. where he would build the city of Samaria and make it the new capital of Israel because It was easily defended and centrally located. God gave the prophet Micah a vision concerning Samaria's fall around 750 B.C.

"Therefore I will make Samaria as an heap of the field, and as plantings of a vineyard: and I will pour down the stones thereof into the valley, and I will discover the foundations thereof." (Micah 1:6). In this 1 verse we are given 4 very specific predictions concerning Samaria.

1. Samaria would fall. Remember Samaria was a walled city atop a great hill, it would be difficult to be overtake. So Stoner placed the odds of Samaria falling at 1:4

2. Samaria will become a heap of the field. Stoner placed the odds at 1:5

3. Samaria will be occupied by vineyards. How often are the ruins of a major city turned into a vineyard? Stoner places the odds at 1:100.

4. The stones from Samaria's mighty walls would be thrown down the hill into the valley. Stoner places the odds at 1:10.

5. Samaria's foundation would be discovered. Stoner placed the odds at 1:2.

The city of Samaria changed hands many times in its history, it was ultimately destroyed by the Hasmanean John Hyrcanus in 108 B.C. It would flourish somewhat as a Roman Province but would never again be a political power. Today Samaria is best known for its many vineyards as well as its ancient stones located in the valley below. all just as Micah had prophesied over 2750 years ago. The odds of all 5 of Micah's prophecies concerning Samaria would all come to pass would be 1: 40,000.[8]

These 4 prophecies concerning the fall of the 4 major cities Nineveh, Tyre, Babylon, and Samaria, are all highly unlikely to have come to pass when taken individually but when taking all 4 prophecies together, the chances that 1 book would correctly predict the fall of all 4 cities in such great detail is astronomical. In fact using Stoner's probability principle the odds of every prophecy concerning these 4 ancient cities coming true is 1:12,000,000,000,000!

The prophecies of Daniel that have been fulfilled. Daniel is considered to be the greatest prophet in the Old Testament. The book of Daniel is one that has been studied by thousands of biblical scholars. Daniel's prophecies are so accurate that critics only response is that Daniel never wrote the book that bears his name. Critics are forced to assume that the amazing predictions made in Daniel were written after the fact. The Dead Sea Scrolls have proven that the book of Daniel was written before 150 B.C. and it seems more than reasonable to accept the fact that the prophet Daniel actually wrote the book that bears his name.

No greater proof is needed than that of Jesus who said this in *"When ye therefore shall see the abomination of desolation, spoken of by Daniel the prophet..."* (Matt.24:15). It is clear that Jesus accepted Daniel as a legitimate prophet.[9]

Daniel steps into the stage as a great prophet when he is able to interpret King Nebuchadnezzar's dream. *"Thou, O King, sawest, and behold a great image. This great image, whose brightness was excellent, stood before thee; and the form thereof was terrible. This image's head was of fine gold, his breast and his arms of silver, his belly and his thighs of brass. His legs of Iron, his feet part of iron and part of clay. Thou sawest till that a stone was cut out without hands, which smote the image upon his feet that were of iron and clay, and brake them to pieces...and the stone that smote the image became a great mountain, and filled the whole Earth."* (Daniel 2:31-35).

Years later Daniel would have a similar dream of 4 beasts rising from the sea. *"And 4 great beasts came up from the sea, diverse one from another. The 1st was like a lion, and had eagle's wings: I beheld till the wings thereof were plucked, and it was lifted up from the earth, and made stand upon the feet as a man, and a man's heart was given to it. And behold another beast, a 2nd, like to a bear, and it raised up itself on one side, and it had 3 ribs in the mouth of it between the teeth of it...After this I beheld, and lo another, like a leopard, which had upon the back of it 4 wings of a fowl; the beast had also 4 heads; and dominion was given to it...and behold a 4th beast, dreadful and terrible, and strong exceedingly; and it had great iron teeth: it devoured and brake in pieces, and stamped the residue with the feet of it: and it was diverse from all the beasts that were before it; and it had 10 horns."* (Daniel 7:3-6).

When you take both dreams and there interpretations then you watch how world history unfolded from around 600 B.C. when Daniel interpreted these dreams until Rome's rise to power in 322 B.C. it is impossible to ignore the similarities.

Babylon was the world's greatest nation in Daniel's day. Daniel had a unique perspective of Babylon as King Nebuchadnezzar's closest advisor. Babylon is represented in Nebuchadnezzar's dream as the statue's golden head and in Daniel's dream as a lion with eagle's wings. Babylon rose to power after its King Nebopaias conquered Nineveh in 612 B.C. in 605 B.C. Babylon defeated Egypt, and in 586 B.C. Babylon captured Jerusalem. Babylon became a lavish empire with its hanging gardens & golden statues. There were golden statues of winged lions guarding the gates of its royal palaces. There is no doubt that Daniel was referring to Babylon in his description of the great statues head of pure gold and a lion with eagle's wings. While Babylon grew in wealth & culture the Persians and Medes were growing in military power. In October of 539 B.C. Babylon fell to the Persians and Medes.

The Persians and Medes ruled the World from 539 B.C. until 331 B.C. They are represented in Nebuchadnezzar's dream by the breast and arms of silver and in Daniel's dream by the bear raised on one side with 3 ribs in its mouth. In 559 B.C. Cyrus the great took over Persia & united with the Medes and overthrew Babylon as the world's greatest power in 539 B.C. The relationship between Persia and the Medes is represented by the bear raised up to one side which reflects how while Persia & the Medes were partners it was clear that Persia was greater.

The 3 ribs represent the 3 powers which were defeated by the Persians and Medes which were Egypt, Assyria, and Babylon.

The Persians and Medes were represented by the torso and arms of silver which represent the 2 arms of power of Persia and the Medes. It is made of silver which is less precious than the golden head of Babylon. While Persia was militarily superior to Babylon it was much less cultured than the Babylonians. The Persian Empire fell in 331 B.C. when Alexander the Great defeated King Darius III making Greece the greatest power in the world.[10]

The Greeks rose to world power very quickly under the leadership of their young and powerful Alexander the Great. In Nebuchadnezzar's dream Greece is represented by the belly & thighs of Brass and in Daniel's dream Greece is represented by the swift leopard with 4 wings and 4 heads. Alexander the Great was son of Philip of Macedon who conquered Greece in the Peloponnesian Wars. Alexander became leader of Greece in 336 B.C. and by 331 B.C. he had defeated Persia, destroyed the port city of Tyre, and began construction of the great city of Alexandria in Egypt. According to Jewish historian Josephus Alexander the Great spared the city of Jerusalem after reading Daniel's prophecies concerning him. He also made plans to rebuild the ancient city of Babylon in 323 B.C. but died suddenly at the age of 32. After his death the empire was divided by Alexander's 4 generals.

 Ptolemy took Egypt, Seleucus took Syria, Cassander took Macedonia, and Lysimachus took Asia Minor, this is obviously pictured by the 4 wings and 4 heads of the Leopard. Of course the leopard pictures the speed of which Greece had become the World's greatest power in 7 years. Greece was also pictured by the belly & thighs of brass in that like brass it may appear elegant but is in no way as refined as the Gold which pictured the culture of Babylon or even the silver of Persia.[10]

The Roman Empire is represented in Nebuchadnezzar's dream by the legs of Iron and feet of iron and clay and by the terrible beast with iron teeth and 10 horns. Rome is founded by Romulas in 753 B.C. but does not become a world leader until Rome defeats the Samnites in 290 B.C. making all of Italy under Roman rule. Peace would not last long as in 264 B.C the Punic wars begin with Carthage which lasted 120 years until 146 B.C. and Rome truly becomes the World's greatest empire. In 63 B.C. Rome took over Judea and destroyed the temple in Jerusalem as Jesus himself predicted in A.D 70. Over the years Rome expands its control into Egypt, Asia Minor, and especially into Europe. In fact Rome begins to gravitate towards Europe which is represented by the 10 toes of iron and clay. As Rome expands it weakens and the legs of solid iron becomes 10 toes of iron mixed with clay making the entire statue weak. Rome is divided into Eastern and Western Empires in 395 A.D. and in 476 A.D. the Western Empire is taken by Odoacer and Rome is never the world empire it once was.

Rome is depicted in *Nebuchadnezzar's* dream as legs of iron which pictures the might of the Roman army. Unlike the Golden culture of Babylon, or the shiny but weak brass of Greece, the Roman Empire is depicted by Iron which is not flashy but is strong and the legs picture how the Roman Empire spread far and wide. Daniel pictures the Roman Empire as a beast with iron teeth that tear apart its enemies. As far as the early church is concerned Rome was certainly a monster as it tortured the early church.

The stone not carved with hands is of course Jesus Christ who ultimately outlasted the mighty Roman Empire despite the severe tribulation with which the church underwent under Roman Rule. Consider how Nero sent 1000's of Christians to their deaths to the amusement of the crowds at the colesium. In 250 A.D. Decius orders an empire wide persecution of all Christians, despite this there are over 15 million Christians by 300 A.D. despite the severe persecution. In 303 A.D. Diocletian and Maximian order all churches to be burned and 1000's of Christians are killed but in 313 A.D. Consantinople institutes the Edict of Milan making Christianity legal throughout the Roman Empire. In 380 A.D. Theodosius makes Christianity only religion in Rome. Today Christianity is the world's largest religion while the Roman Empire has long since been a world power.[10]

The prophecies of Daniel are incredibly detailed and accurate, much more so than the prophecies of Nostradamus!

The Eastern Gate prophecy. One of the most remarkable Bible prophecies concerns the Eastern Gate of the wall that surrounds the city of Jerusalem. In 1 Chronicles 11:4-7 we see where King David captures the city of Jerusalem from the Jebusites and makes Jerusalem the capital of Israel. *"And David and all Israel went to Jerusalem...where the Jebusites were the inhabitants of the land...David took the castle of Zion, which is the city of David...and David dwelt in the castle, therefore they called it the city of David."* We know David ruled Israel from 1015 B.C. to 985 B.C. In 586 B.C. Jerusalem is destroyed by the Babylonians, Solomon's temple as well as the city walls were destroyed. Nehemiah rebuilds the walls of Jerusalem in 445 B.C. and gives a detailed account of the rebuilding of the ten gates of Jerusalem's wall.

These 10 gates give a beautiful picture of God's wonderful plan to redeem mankind.

1. **The Sheep Gate:** *"Then Eliashib the high priest rose up with his brethren the priest and them builded the sheep gate; they sanctified it and set up the doors of it."* (Nehemiah 3:1).The sheep gate is the very 1st gate to be rebuilt, it is the only gate to be sanctified by priest. It is also the only gate to have no locks on it as it was the gate where the people would bring their sacrifices. The Sheep gate symbolizes Calvary where Jesus became the Lamb of God sacrificed for our sin. The fact that the sheep gate is never locked illustrates how the door of salvation is always open.

2. **The Fish Gate:** *"But the fish gate did the sons of Hassenaah build...and beams...locks...and bars thereof."* (Nehemiah 3:3). The fish gate symbolizes that Jesus calls us to be fishers of men.

3. **The Old Gate:** *"Moreover the old gate repaired Jehoida the son of Paseah...they laid the beams...locks...and bars thereof."* (Nehemiah 3:6). The old gate is where merchants set up their tables and sales their goods. The old gate symbolizes our old life of sin which often seems desirable.

4. **The Valley Gate:** *"The valley gate repaired Hanun, and the inhabitants of Zanoah; they built it...beams...locks...and bars thereof."* (Nehemiah 3:13). This gate symbolizes the trials and tribulations of life.

5. **The Dung Gate:** *"But the dung gate repaired Malchiah...he built it...doors...locks...and bars thereof."* (Nehemiah 3:14). This is the gate that leads out to hades where the dead were burned along with the city's trash. The dung gate represents all of man's righteousness which leads to Hell.

6. **The Fountain Gate:** *"But the gate of the fountain repaired Shallun...he built it, and covered it, and set up the doors thereof...locks...and bars thereof, and the wall of the pool of Siloah by the king's garden..."* (Nehemiah 3:15). The Fountain gate is only accessed by the king and his men this is why it is covered. The fountain gate symbolizes the Holy Spirit which fills our hearts like a fountain. The fact it is accessed by the King illustrates the importance of allowing the Holy Spirit to dwell as King of our hearts.

7. **The Water Gate:** *"Moreover the Nethinims dwelt in Ophel, unto the place over against the water gate toward the east..."* (Nehemiah 3:26). The water gate is the only gate that needed no repairs. It represents God's Holy Word which sustains our spiritual lives just as water sustains our physical lives. God's word is perfect and needs no rebuilding.

8. **The Horse Gate:** *"From above the horse gate repaired the priests, every one over against his house..."* (Nehemiah 3:28).The horse gate was the widest gate on Jerusalem's wall as it was through this gate the horses would go into battle. The horse Gate represents spiritual warfare.

9. **The Eastern Gate:** *"...after him repaired also Shemaiah the son of Shechaniah, the keeper of the east gate."* (Nehemiah 3:29). The Eastern gate repairs are not detailed which may reveal how it will remain shut. The Eastern Gate led to the temple and It is through the Eastern gate that Jesus will enter Jerusalem as Messiah.

10. **The Miphkad Gate:**" *After him repaired Maichiah the goldsmiths son...over against the gate Miphkad.*"(Nehemiah 3:31). Miphkad is the Hebrew word for judgment and symbolizes God's judgment.[10]

Ezekiel is given an interesting prophecy concerning the Eastern gate. *"Then he brought me back the way of the gate of the outward sanctuary which looked toward the east; and it was shut. Then said the Lord unto me; this gate shall be shut, it shall not be opened, and no man shall enter in by it; because the Lord, the God of Israel, hath entered in by it, therefore it shall be shut. It is for the prince...he shall enter by the way of the porch of that gate."* (Ezekiel 44:1-3). The book of Ezekiel was written around 575 B.C. and Nehemaih rebuilt the city walls around 440 B.C. and here the eastern gate is opened. In Jesus day the Eastern Gate is open and leads to the temple. In A.D. 70 Rome take control of Jerusalem until 636 A.D. when the Arabs take control of Jerusalem and in 1099 A.D. they have the eastern gate sealed to prevent the Jewish Messiah from coming which ironically helped fulfill scripture. The Arabs also build a grave in front of the sealed eastern gate to prevent the Jewish Messiah from entering the eastern gate. Hundreds of years later The Turks of the Ottoman Empire take over Jerusalem. Ottoman Sultan Suleiman the magnificent rebuilds the crumbling walls of Jerusalem around 1535 A.D.

He only rebuilds 8 of the original 10 gates. Oddly enough he rebuilds walls but never unseals the Eastern gate. My question is why would you rebuild 8 gates and not unseal the Eastern Gate? No one can answer that question today but the fact remains that of the original 10 gates Nehemiah rebuilt only one is sealed up just as scripture predicted it would be...the Eastern Gate.

We know the Eastern Gate is sealed today but the interesting thing is that there were a couple of times in history where it was nearly opened. On December 12th 1917 Hussein Bey Al Husayni, a charismatic mayor of Jerusalem, attempted to pacify the 10,000 Jews that occupied Jerusalem at the time by opening the Eastern Gate. Before the gate was opened British General Edmund Allenby captured Jerusalem thwarting any attempt to have the gate opened.[11]

Jordanian King Hussein had often stated that he would defy the Bible by having the eastern gate opened. He had planned to do it but on June 7th 1967 he lost control of Jerusalem and never was able to open the eastern gate. Even today Israel's housing ministry plans on opening the eastern gate but Palestine controls the eastern gate making it impossible for this to happen. What are the odds that of the 10 gates built by Nehemiah only the eastern gate would be sealed shut despite attempts to open it? [12]

The history of Israel fulfills Biblical prophecy.

While on Biblical prophecy I want to show the most convincing of all biblical prophecy which is the fact that the nation of Israel even exists today. When you look at the history of the Jews over the past 100 years it is remarkable. From 1917 when the British took control of Jerusalem from the Arabs Jews have been flocking back to Jerusalem fulfilling Biblical prophecy.

"And it shall come to pass in that day, that the Lord shall set his hand again the 2nd time to recover the remnant of his people, which shall be left...and he shall set up an ensign for the nations, and shall assemble the outcasts of Israel, and gather together the dispersed of Judah from the four corners of the earth" (Isaiah 11:11-12).

In 1917 when the British gained control of Jerusalem there were only 10,000 Jews in the city, by 1948 there were over 650,000 Jews in Jerusalem. It is on May 14th 1948 Israel once again becomes a nation. Think about it, for almost 2000 years Israel did not exist. Thousands of Jews were scattered all over the world and then from 1933 to 1945 Nazi Germany slaughtered nearly 6 million Jews.

It seemed as though the Jews would never again occupy Jerusalem...until May 14th 1948 Israel becomes a nation which seems to be answering a question found in *"Can a country be born in a day or a nation be brought forth in a moment?"* (Isaiah 66:8). The answer is ...yes it can and yes it did. Even though it is highly unlikely, especially for the nation of Israel which had been scattered and persecuted, yet it happened. In 1948 there were 650,000 Jews, today there are over 6 million Jews in Israel.[13]

The Prophecies of Jesus Birth. When you stop to consider the number of prophecies in the Bible that have already come true and you realize that no other book has ever made even one similar prophecy then you must ask yourself, could it be that the Bible is truly God's word? Let's turn our attention to Jesus Christ and the prophecies that he alone fulfilled.

The very first prophetic verse in the Bible is *"And I will put enmity between thee and the woman, and between thy seed* and her seed; it shall bruise thy head, and thou shall bruise his heel." (Genesis 3:15). It is referred to as the proto-evangelium which means 1st Gospel. This one verse predicts that there will be a messiah, he will be a male, and that he will be born. From the very beginning God had planned to redeem mankind by sending his Son as our savior.[13]

As far as specific prophecies go there are many which concern Jesus birth. Here are a few.

1. *"Therefore the Lord himself shall give you a sign; Behold, a virgin shall conceive, and bear a son, and call his name Immanuel."* (Isaiah 7:14). The Messiah would be born of a virgin. *"Then said Mary unto the angel, how shall this be, seeing I know not a man?"* (Luke 1:34). Mary confessed that she was a virgin when the angel Gabriel told her she was pregnant with a son which would save the world.

2. **(Isaiah 7:14)** The Messiah would be named Immanuel. *"Behold a virgin shall be with child, and shall bring forth a son and they shall call his name Emmanuel, which being interpreted is, God with us."* (Matt. 1:23). I find it interesting that some claim that Jesus never claimed to be God yet he was given the name *"God with us"* indicating his diety.

3. *"But thou, Bethlehem Ephratah, though thou be little among the thousands of Judah, yet out of thee shall he come forth unto me that is to be ruler in Israel; whose goings forth have been from of old, from everlasting"* (Micah 5:2). Bethlehem is known as the house of bread which would be the birthplace of the one that would become the bread of life. Bethlehem is also the birthplace of King David. David is considered to be Israel's greatest

King but Jesus would become King of King's. *"And Joseph also went up from Galilee, out of the city of Nazareth, into Judea, unto the city of David, which is called Bethlehem...and she brought forth her firstborn son."* (Luke 2:4-7). Jesus was born in the small town of Bethlehem just as the Bible predicted. Critics often point out that if Jesus was born in Bethlehem why is he known as Jesus of Nazareth if he was born in Bethlehem. The scripture seems to explain this quite well as it records that Joseph and Mary left Nazareth to travel to Bethlehem to be taxed.

This is in no way unusual, I was born in Phenix City Alabama and later moved to Carrollton Georgia. Since I grew up in Carrollton most people know that I am from Carrollton Georgia even though I was born in Phenix City Alabama. The fact that the Bible describes Jesus as being born in Bethlehem yet is known as Jesus of Nazareth is even more believable not less.

4.   *"Now the Lord had said unto Abram, get thee out of thy country...unto a land I will show thee. And I will make of thee a great nation, and I will bless thee, and make thy name great; and thou shalt be a blessing...and in thee shall all the families of the earth be blessed."* (Gen. 12:1-3). This is known as the Abrahamic Covenant and for Jews it is the covenant that makes them the children of God. However this Abrahamic Covenant is meant for all the families of the earth and it refers to Jesus. *"The book of the generation of Jesus Christ, the Son of David, the son of Abraham."* (Matt. 1:1). The New Testament begins with the genealogy of Jesus which begins with Abraham. It is significant that Jesus is a descendant of Abraham in that it connects Jesus with the Abrahamic Covenant.

5. *"Now therefore so shalt thou say unto my servant David...I took thee from a sheepcote...to be ruler over my people, over Israel? And thine house and thy kingdom shall be established forever before thee, thy throne shall be established forever."* (2 Samuel 7:8;16). Jesus would come from the line of David which he did according to his genealogy found in Matthew 1:1.

6. *"The Kings of Tarshish and of the Isles shall bring presents: the kings of Sheba and Seba shall offer gifts. Yea, all the kings shall fall down before him: all nations shall serve him."* (Psalm 72:10-11). One of the amazing qualities of Biblical prophecy is how it does not simply predict one historical event it often refers to more than one event and often can be true in numerous times past, present, and future. This particular prophecy refers to the wise men who visited Jesus as a young child as well as a time in the future when every king will bow down and worship Jesus as King of Kings and Lord of Lords. *"Now when Jesus was born in Bethlehem of Judea in the days of Herod the king, behold there came wise men from the east to Jerusalem. And when they were come into the house, they saw the young child with Mary his mother, and fell down, and worshipped him...they presented unto him gifts: gold, frankincense and myrrh."* (Matt. 2:1;11).

Not only did the wise men worship the child Jesus they brought 3 prophetic gifts: Gold which pictures the glory of Jesus as God's son. Frankincense, which has many uses but it was considered medicinal in Jesus day, a very expensive medicine that if applied to a scorpion sting or rash would heal the wound. This pictures the healing nature of Jesus life as well as the power of his shed blood to heal man's sin. Myrrh also had many uses but its primary use in Jesus day was as a powerful perfume which was commonly used to prepare dead bodies. Myrrh pictures the Jesus sacrificial death on the cross to save mankind from the sin debt that no man could possibly pay.

7. *"When Israel was a child, then I loved him, and called my son out of Egypt."* (Hosea 11:1). While many Biblical critics claim that these verses refer to Israel's Egyptian captivity or to some other event, if these were the only 2 predictions in the Bibles concerning Jesus then I would be inclined to doubt these prophecies as well. However, when you take the other prophecies and add these it seems reasonable to accept that these verses point to the life of Jesus. Especially when scripture itself claims that it is fulfilled prophecy. *"When he arose, he took the young child and his mother by night, and departed into Egypt. And was there until the death of Herod: that it might be fulfilled which was spoken of the Lord by the prophet, saying, Out of Egypt I have called my son."* (Matt. 2:14-15).

When you take each prophecy alone it seems plausible but when you begin to add up these prophecies concerning Jesus birth and childhood it starts becoming more unlikely that these Bible prophecies would get all this stuff right. How much more specific can you get when you take that Jesus is born in Bethlehem, raised in Nazareth, and fled to Egypt.[13]

Depending on which commentary you believe Jesus fulfilled anywhere from 45 to 353 prophecies in his earthly ministry and it would take a separate book to go over them all. We have already touched on 7 which prophesied Jesus birth let's now focus on 2 amazing scriptures that point so clearly to Jesus Christ that Jewish students are forbidden to read them.

The Prophecies of Jesus found in Isaiah 53.

"For he shall grow up before him as a tender plant, and as a root out of a dry ground: he hath no form nor comeliness: and when we shall see him, there is no beauty that we should desire him. He is despised and rejected of men: a man of sorrows, and acquainted with grief...Surely he hath borne our griefs, and carried our sorrows: yet we did esteem him stricken, smitten of God, and afflicted. But he was wounded for our transgressions, he was bruised for our iniquities: the chastisement of our peace was upon him; and with his stripes we are healed...He was oppressed, and he was afflicted, yet he opened not his mouth: he is brought as a lamb to the slaughter...for the transgression of my people was he stricken. And he made his grave with the wicked, and with the rich in his death; because he had done no violence...Yet it pleased the Lord to bruise him; he hath put him to grief: when thou shalt make his soul an offering for sin...Therefore will I divide him a portion with the great, and he shall divide the spoil with the strong; because he hath poured out his soul unto death; and he was numbered with the transgressors; and he bare the sin of many, and made intercession for the transgressors." (Isaiah 53)

Before diving into Isaiah 53 remember that this passage was written around 700 B.C., before the Dead Sea Scrolls were found Biblical skeptics assumed that Isaiah 53 must have been written after Jesus had been crucified, but when a full scroll of Isaiah was found and dated to 150 B.C. there is no doubt that this passage was written well before Jesus was even born.[13]

Jesus is like a root out of a dry ground in that He is nothing less than Holy God who brought life into a dry sinful world. Notice Jesus own words concerning his Godly nature. *"And now, O*

Father, glorify thou me with thine own self with the glory which I had with thee before the world was." (Luke 17:5). For all the critics who suggest Jesus never claimed to be God what do you call what Jesus says here? Jesus is indeed a root out of a dry ground.

Jesus was despised and rejected. *"And he came to Nazareth, where he had been brought up...and stood up for to read...And all they in the synagogue, when they heard these things, were filled with wrath. And rose up, and thrust him out of the city."* (Luke 4:16;28-29). Jesus was kicked out of his own hometown.

Jesus was a man of sorrow, acquainted with grief. *"My soul is exceeding sorrowful, even into death."* (Matt.26:38). The reasons for Jesus sorrow and grief are many. 1st Man's sinful condition causes Jesus to be sorrowful. Next, man's pride which keeps so many from coming to salvation causes Jesus to grieve. In this context, Jesus was sorrowful because he was about to become sin and receive the punishment that we all deserve. God the father would soon turn his back on his only begotten son.

Jesus bore our grief and carried our sorrows. Listen to Jesus words here. *"Come unto me, all ye that labour and are heavy laden, and I will give you rest. Take my yoke upon you, and learn of me; for I am meek and lowly in heart: and ye shall find rest unto your souls. For my yoke is easy, and my burden is light."* (Matt.11:28-30). Jesus came to this world in large part to take the heavy burden of our sin on himself because the weight is too much for us to bear.

One of my favorite songs is "Worn" by Tenth Avenue North. I love the words *"my soul seems crushed by the weight of this world and I know that you can give me rest so I cry out with all* that I have left...let me see redemption win, let me know the struggle ends, that you can mend a heart that's frail & torn. I wanna know a song can rise from the ashes of a broken life and all that's dead inside an be reborn, cause I'm worn..."[14]   Jesus bears the burden of our sin.

The Jewish leadership saw the crucifixion of Jesus as God's punishment on this blasphemer. He was rightly afflicted in their eyes. Notice the description of the crowd gathered watching Jesus as he hung on that old rugged cross. *"They that passed by reviled him, wagging their heads saying...save thyself if thou be the Son of God, come down from the cross. Likewise also the chief priests mocking him, with the scribes and elders...If he be the King of Israel, let him now come down from the cross, and we will believe him..."* (Matt.27:39-42).

The truth is that they were absolutely right, in that had Jesus came off the cross they would have believed and followed Jesus anywhere...The problem was that it was not God's will nor was it the reason Jesus came to earth. Jesus purpose for coming to the earth was totally missed by many Jews then and continues to be missed by many today. Most people have no idea how God in the flesh would allow himself to be crucified with petty thieves on a cross. It simply makes no sense. There seems to be no glory or dignity in the cross. The cross still offends many today.

Jesus was wounded for our transgressions, he was bruised for our iniquities. The chastisement which we deserved was placed on him. By the blood of Jesus we are healed. Paul describes this beautifully in *"God commendeth his love toward us, in that, while we were yet sinners, Christ died for us. Much more then, being now justified by his blood, we shall be saved from wrath through him."* (Romans 5:8-9). What Jesus did for you and I on Calvary cannot be overstated. We were sinners, undeserving of God's love yet even so God demonstrated his love for you and I through his Son Jesus Christ who shed his blood for us all. Willmington puts it this way *"Christ experienced our hell that we might experience his heaven"* [15] Then there are the wonderful words of one of my favorite hymns by Robert Lowry. *"What can wash away my sins? Nothing but the blood of Jesus..."*[16]

Jesus stood silent before his accusers, like a lamb being led to the slaughter. *"When Herod saw Jesus...He questioned him with many words; but he answered him nothing."* (Luke 23:8-9). Jesus went through 7 separate trials, all of which were illegal and highly unusual. After his arrest he was led to the home of Annas the High priest, he then faced Caiaphas, then the Sanhedrin, then he was brought before Pilate in the courtyard, Then he was brought before Herod, then finally back to Pilate. Throughout each of these trials Jesus never defended himself, rather he was like a lamb being led to the slaughter.

Jesus was crucified with thieves yet he was buried with the wealthy. *"Then were there two thieves crucified with him, one on the right hand, and another on the left."* (Matt.27:38). *"When the even was come, there came a rich man of Arimathaea, named Joseph... He went to Pilate and begged the body of Jesus...Joseph had taken the body, he wrapped it in a clean linen cloth...and laid it in his own new tomb."* (Matt.27:57-60). Here we have the most unlikely pairings of prophecy. How the Messiah would make his grave with the wicked and be with the rich in death...this would be highly unlikely yet that is exactly what happened to Jesus. This would have been extremely hard to plan or to fake. The most reasonable explanation is found in scripture.

Many have argued over who really killed Jesus. While we all share in the blame and there are many who are culpable such as Pilate, Caiaphas, Judas Iscariot, the angry crowd who yelled crucify him, crucify him... the truth is that Jesus crucifixion was God's pleasure. *"Him being delivered by the determinate counsel and foreknowledge of God, ye have taken by wicked hands have crucified and slain."* (Acts 2:23). Why did Jesus die on the cross? The answer is that it pleased God. Jesus chose to go to the cross my friend. There is no power on this earth that could have killed Jesus if he did not want to be killed. The wonderful truth is that Jesus willingly placed himself on the cross in obedience to God the Father so that we might be saved. I love what Jesus says here *"Therefore doth my father love me, because I lay down my life, that I might take it again. No man taketh it from me, but I lay it down of myself, I have power to lay it down, and I have the power to take it again."* (John 10:17-18).

Jesus bare the sins of many, and made intercession for the transgressors. *"For God so loved the world, that he gave his only begotten son, that whosoever believeth in him should not perish, but have everlasting life. For God sent not his son into the world to condemn the world; but that the world through him might be saved."* (John 3:16-17). If you spend any time on the internet looking at the things skeptics say concerning Biblical prophecy it really makes you wonder how they explain away Isaiah 53. Jesus uniquely fulfills Isaiah 53.

It is no wonder the Ethiopian Eunich got saved once Phillip explained what he was reading. It is also no wonder that Jewish religious leaders do not want any Jew reading Isaiah 53. The real question is what do you say? Is Jesus the Messiah that is described here in Isaiah? If he is, then there is no other way besides Jesus Christ to be saved. Isaiah 53 defies skeptics. It is so descriptive of the life of Jesus it cannot be explained away. Skeptics long assumed it was written well after Jesus had lived. The Dead Sea Scrolls proved that Isaiah was written before 150 B.C., well before the life of Jesus.[17]

The Prophecy of Jesus crucifixion found in Psalm 22.

If Isaiah 53 is not enough to convince you that Jesus is the Son of God and the only way to be saved let's take a look at Psalm 22. This Psalm is written by David around 1000 B.C. making it 1000 years before Jesus lived. Even more astounding is the fact that the Persians are credited for 1st using crucifixion as a means for capital punishment around 700 B.C., some 300 years after David wrote this Psalm. This Psalm is the most complete description of Jesus crucifixion in the Bible. It seems as though David was given an intimate look into the very heart of Jesus as he hung on the cross. David refers to all 7 quotes the Gospels record Jesus saying on the cross.[18]

"My God My God, why hast thou forsaken me" (Psalm 22:1). Jesus quotes this very passage from the cross in Matthew 27:46. I remember watching Mel Gibson's *The Passion of the Christ"* and identifying with the enormous physical pain that Jesus endured as he was beaten, scourged, and ultimately crucified. It was so hard to watch that I doubt I can watch it again. The truth is that the physical pain was the easy part, it was the spiritual and emotional part that caused Jesus to cry out *"My God, My God, Why hast thou forsaken me."* It was on the cross that Jesus took on our sin, he became sin, and his heavenly Father who he had been with for eternity past turned his back on his only son. The only person who deserves God's love becomes the only one to take all of God's judgment: While we who deserve God's

Judgment, receive God's amazing grace and love. We receive this grace and love though the blood of Jesus Christ and because of Jesus precious blood we will never experience the awful feeling Jesus felt as he hung on the cross...separation from God.

"But I am a worm, and no man, a reproach of men, and despised of the people. All that see me laugh me to scorn they shoot out the lip...." (Psalm 22:6-7). Here David describes how Jesus must have felt while hanging on the cross as the crowd laughs at him, curses him, the Son of God had become a worm a reproach of men, and despised of the people. While he felt these things he still showed his great love for the men and women who were laughing at him, cursing him, as he looked down from the cross and said these wonderful words. *"Father, forgive them ; for they know not what they do."* (Luke 23:34). Even though we all have chosen to sin and go against God's Word, Jesus still loves us and forgives us.

"But thou art he that took me out of the womb, thou didst make me hope when I was upon my mother's breasts. I was cast upon thee from the womb: thou art my God from my mother's belly." (Psalm 22:9-10). As Jesus looks at the crowd he turns his attention to his mother Mary. *"When Jesus therefore saw his mother...he saith unto his mother "Woman behold thy Son". Then saith he to the disciple, "Behold thy mother!"* (John 19:26-27). We often talk about how Jesus is 100% God, but here we see him as 100% human. There is nothing more human than having a special love for your mother. Mary was a loving Godly mother who understood better than anyone else in the crowd that her son was nothing less than the Son of God.

"I am poured out like water, and all my bones are out of joint: my heart is like wax; it is melted in the midst of my bowels. My strength is dried up like a potsherd; and my tongue cleaveth to my jaws; and thou hast brought me into the dust of death." (Psalm 22:14-15). As you read this remember it was written by David who probably had no idea about crucifixion. Medical doctors have studied the effects of crucifixion and what David describes here is totally in line with what the medical doctors describe. Dr. Pierre Barbet, a French surgeon who has done exhaustive historical and experimental research and has written extensively on the subject.

"As He pushes Himself upward to avoid this stretching torment, He places His full weight on the nail through His feet. Again there is the searing agony of the nail tearing through the nerves between the metatarsal bones of the feet. At this point, as the arms fatigue, great waves of cramps sweep over the muscles, knotting them in deep, relentless, throbbing pain. With these cramps comes the inability to push Himself upward. Hanging by his arms, the pectoral muscles are paralyzed and the intercostal muscles are unable to act. Air can be drawn into the lungs, but cannot be exhaled. Jesus fights to raise Himself in order to get even one short breath. Finally, carbon dioxide builds up in the lungs and in the blood stream and the cramps partially subside. Spasmodically, he is able to push Himself upward to exhale and bring in the life-giving oxygen. Jesus experienced hours of limitless pain, cycles of twisting, joint-rending cramps, intermittent partial asphyxiation, searing pain where tissue is torn from His lacerated back as He moves up and down against the rough timber. Then another agony begins -- a terrible crushing pain deep in the chest as the pericardium slowly fills with serum and begins to compress the heart".[19]

It is at this point Jesus says *"I Thirst"* (John 19:28). We have discussed in detail the physical condition that Jesus was in as he hung on the cross. While I'm certain that he was physically thirsty here I believe the words "I thirst" have a deeper and powerful meaning. Remember back in the Garden of Gethsemane when Jesus said in *"Father, if thou be willing, remove this cup from me nevertheless not my will, but thine be done."* (Luke 22:42).

 He was asking his Father, God, that if there be any other way to bring salvation to sinful man then Jesus said let's do that. People say if you believe Jesus is the only way to Heaven then you are narrow minded. I would say if there was another way to heaven then God is the most unloving, uncaring father ever. The truth is there is no other way. So Jesus went to Calvary's cross and as he hung there with the weight of our sin on his shoulders and as he was shedding his blood he says *"I Thirst"* Is there anything else for me to do? Is there any more sin? If so I thirst for it. Jesus desired to drink every last drop from the cup, there would be no sin unaccounted for. Jesus drank every drop of that awful cup and thirsted for more because He loves you and I.

 "...They pierced my hands and my feet...they part my garments among them, and cast lots upon my vesture." (Psalm 22:16-18). Here we see the amazing accuracy of David's prophecy as he describes in detail the unique events of Jesus crucifixion. Many skeptics say that Jesus orchestrated things in such a way as to make it seem as though he was fulfilling prophecy. How could Jesus orchestrate the Roman soldiers casting lots at his feet? How could David even know any of these details?

"But be not thou far from me, O Lord: O my strength, haste thee to help me." (Psalm 22:19).Jesus once again turns his attention

back to his heavenly Father before he breaths his last breath. *"And when Jesus had cried with a loud voice, he said "Father, into thy hands I commend my spirit."* (Luke 23:46).

"...In the midst of the congregation will I praise thee. Ye that fear the Lord praise him...For he hath not despised nor abhorred the affliction of the afflicted...but when he cried unto him, he heard...The meek shall eat and be satisfied: they shall praise the Lord that seek him; your heart shall live forever."(Psalm 22:22-26). David alludes to the thief on the cross who cries out to Jesus for salvation. Jesus responds *"Verily I say unto thee, today shalt thou be with me in paradise."* (Luke 23:43).

The 2 thieves hanging on either side of Jesus were unfit to live according to Roman law. Yet Jesus offers them eternal life. One accepts, one rejects...what a picture of how salvation works. Jesus offers salvation to all, but not all accept the invitation. There are those that try to say a loving God would not allow anyone to go to Hell. The truth is God wants none to go to Hell and He offers salvation to all mankind but he does not force it on anyone. It is offered for all but some will pride fully reject this wonderful gift of amazing grace. What about you today? Will you accept the offer of Amazing Grace which has been paid for by Jesus blood which he shed on the cross?

"All the ends of the world shall remember and turn to the Lord: and all the kindred's of the nations shall worship before thee." (Psalm 22:27). Some may say, how can you know that David is referring to Jesus crucifixion here? What is the one single event in all of history that would cause the world to remember and turn to God? It is the cross of Jesus Christ. *"And being found in fashion as a man, he humbled himself, and became obedient unto death, even the death of the cross. Wherefore God also*

hath highly exalted him, and given him a name which is above every name: That at the name of Jesus every knee should bow..." (Philippians 2:8-10).

Those that try and say Jesus is simply a good man, a great teacher, or a loving prophet they will one day acknowledge Jesus as the one and only Son of God who sacrificed himself on the old rugged cross and is now placed above all names. And one day every tongue will confess him as King of Kings and Lord of Lord's.

"They shall come, and shall declare his righteousness unto a people that shall be born, that he hath done this." (Psalm 22:31). I can't help but notice David's words at the end of this remarkable Psalm as he explains that it was written *unto a people that shall be born.* It seems to me that David understood that this particular Psalm was meant for those yet to be born...for you and I. David also hints to Jesus final words as he ends with the words *"He hath done this"* Jesus final words on the cross are *"It is finished"* (John 19:30).

Jesus is saying that there is absolutely nothing left to do. There is nothing that anyone can add to what Jesus finished on the cross. When we try to add anything to what Jesus finished on the cross we are removing our trust in Jesus work on the cross and placing our trust in our own ability. Our pride has a hard time accepting the fact that Jesus did it all on the cross with no assistance from anyone. The wonderful thing is that we are able to rest in Jesus finished work on the cross.[20]

Revelation as it relates to end time prophecies. I am not going to go into much detail into the end time's prophecies of Revelation, that is the subject for another book, but I do want to give a brief description of what Revelations reveals about the end of days. When studying the book it is important to understand how the book of Revelation is laid out.

Chapter 1: John begins Revelation by revealing the glorified Christ. John wanted to make sure the reader understood that Jesus was no longer the humble carpenter but is now the King of Kings.

Chapter 2-3: John describes the 7 churches of Asia Minor.

Chapter 4-5: John is taken to heaven where he describes the throne of God. These chapters coincide with Daniel 7 and 12. It is helpful to understand the tabernacle as it pictures God's heavenly throne.

Chapter 6: John describes the 7 seal judgments which begins the Great Tribulation where the Anti-Christ comes to power.

Chapter 7: Here we have the 1st interlude as John pauses between the 6th and 7th seal judgments and describes the 144,000 Jewish evangelists.

Chapter 8-9: John describes the 7 trumpet judgments.

Chapter 10-11: The 2nd interlude between the 6th and 7th trumpet judgments. John describes 2 witnesses who are killed by the Anti-Christ only to raise 3 ½ days later.

Chapter 12-13: John describes the unholy trinity, the dragon, (Satan), the beast, (anti-Christ), and the prostitute (false prophet). Whose number is 666. I find this particular prophecy interesting in that when I was younger, in the early 80's, many pictured the Anti-Christ painting the number 666 in red on the forehead of those forced to take the mark.

Today we realize this number won't be literally painted on the forehead. It will obviously be a micro-chip with all of your identification numbers, banking numbers, and other personal information on it. Without this number in your forehead you will not be able to purchase anything. This is obvious today, but 50 years ago it was a stretch to imagine, 500 years ago it made no sense at all. How did the Apostle John living 2000 years ago come up with placing a number on the forehead as a mark of the Beast? Once again we see how amazing Biblical prophecy is.

Chapter 14: John skips ahead in time and describes the victory of the lamb and the 144,000.

Chapter 15: Heaven pauses and gets ready for God's final 7 bowl judgments.

Chapter 16: John describes the 7 bowl judgments.

Chapter 17-18: Mystery Babylon rises and falls as well as the unholy trinity.

Chapter 19: John describes the wedding supper of the lamb, Jesus 2nd coming, and his victory over Satan at Armageddon.

Chapter 20: John describes the Millennial Kingdom, when Jesus reigns on Earth for 1000 years. It is during this millennial Kingdom where many unfulfilled Biblical prophecies will finally come true. Here are a few.

"And he shall judge among the nations, and shall rebuke many people: and they shall beat their swords to plowshares, and their spears into pruning hooks; nation shall not lift sword against nation, neither shall they learn war anymore." (Isaiah 2:4) This prophecy has never come true, and won't come true

until Jesus returns from heaven and establishes his 1000 year reign of peace described here in Isaiah.

"The desert shall rejoice, and blossom as the rose...the eyes of the blind shall be opened, and the ears of the deaf shall be unstopped...and the parched ground shall become a pool." (Isaiah 35:1-7) After the natural disasters of the great tribulation the earth as we know it today will be drastically changed in a matter of weeks. Much as the earth was drastically changed in a matter of weeks after the great flood. The earth will become more inhabitable as less than 20% of the Earth's surface in inhabitable today. What if in the millennial kingdom the earth became 50%, or 75% inhabitable? I believe it will. Not only will the earth become more inhabitable, the curse of sin will be removed and there will be no blind or deaf. [21]

"The wolf shall dwell with the lamb, and the leopard shall lie down with the kid, and the calf and the young lion, and the fatling together;...and the suckling child shall play on the hole of the asp...for the earth shall be full of the knowledge of the Lord." (Isaiah 11:6-9) This prophecy has never taken place but it will in the millennial Kingdom. It will be as it was in the Garden of Eden before man had sinned. Imagine petting a lion, or playing with a rattle snake, this will happen during the millennial kingdom. Also understand that while living in a much more inhabitable earth, with no worry of death or disease, we will be able to learn about the nature of God as well as the person of Jesus Christ.

What a day that will be When my Jesus I shall see,
And I look upon His face, The One who saved me by His grace;
When He takes me by the hand And leads me through the
Promised Land, What a day, glorious day that will be.

There'll be no sorrow there, no more burdens to bear,
No more sickness, no pain, no more parting over there;
And forever I will be with the One who died for me,
What a day, glorious day that will be.[22]

Chapter 21-22: John describes the new heaven and new earth as the old heaven and earth are destroyed.

The Rapture of the church.

There are many Christians who do not believe in or fully understand what the Bible teaches about the rapture, in fact there are 3 main views concerning the rapture among Christians, Post-Tribulation , Mid-Tribulation, and Pre-Tribulation believers.

The Post- Tribulation believers do not believe in the rapture, they correctly point out that the word rapture is not mentioned in the Bible. They use this scripture to defend this belief. Matthew 24:29-30 *"Immediately after the tribulation of those days shall the sun be darkened, and the moon shall not give her light, and the stars shall fall from Heaven, and the powers of the heavens shall be shaken. And then shall appear the sign of the son of man in Heaven and then shall all the tribes of the Earth mourn, and they shall see the Son of Man coming in the clouds of heaven with power and great glory."* (Matt. 24:29-30).

Here Jesus himself says that after the tribulation he shall come in the clouds. This seems pretty cut and dry, however it is important that we do not make all of our beliefs around one passage. This is a perfect illustration of the danger in basing your beliefs on one passage to the exclusion of all others. It is certainly true that Jesus will come to Earth after the tribulation, there is no debating this fact. The question seems to be is there any other scriptures that may suggest that Jesus will come to earth before this event?

The Mid-Tribulation believers say that the church will endure the 1st half of the tribulation but will be caught up with the 2 witnesses. They use this scripture to defend this belief. Revelation 11:3-12 here are a few excerpts of this passage " *And I will power unto my 2 witnesses, and they shall prophecy for 2260 days...and when they have finished their testimony, the beast that ascendeth out of the bottomless pit shall make war against them, and shall overcome them, and kill them. And their dead bodies shall lie in the street...3 ½ days...and after 3 ½ days the spirit of life from God entered into them and they stood up on their feet...and they heard a great voice from heaven saying unto them come up hither. And they ascended up to heaven in a cloud."*

Both Daniel and Revelation divide the tribulation into 2 halves, each lasting 3 ½ years. The first half is considered to be the wrath of the anti-Christ who rises to power and causes great tribulation for any who do not worship him. The second half is considered to be much worse as it is the wrath of God on the world who has chosen to follow the anti-Christ. According to those that hold a mid-tribulation view the church will endure the 1st half of the tribulation in which the anti-Christ rules. Those that remain faithful to God and do not worship the Ant-Christ will be called up to heaven with the 2 witnesses. This seems to be reading things into scripture that do not seem to be there, but I can see how they may interpret a mid-tribulation belief.[23]

The Pre- tribulation believers like myself believe that the church will be raptured up before the tribulation. There is a great deal of Biblical evidence to support a pre-tribulation view. One of the best ways to interpret the Bible is to step back and try to get the big picture. In order to do that we must find the purpose of the tribulation. The Bible gives us 3 reasons for the great tribulation.

The first reason that God will send Great Tribulation is to reveal the wickedness of Satan to the world. *"How art thou fallen from heaven O Lucifer, son of the morning, How art thou cut to the ground, which didst weaken the nations. For thou hast said in thine heart I will ascend unto heaven, I will exalt my throne above the stars of God. I will sit also upon the mount of the congregation...I will be like the Most High. Yet thou shall be brought down to Hell."* (Isaiah 14:12-15).

"And the great Dragon was cast out, that old serpent, called the Devil, and Satan, which deceiveth the whole world. He was cast out..." (Rev.12:9). There are many today who see no wrong in doing whatever makes you happy, to get ahead in life. They might look at Lucifer and commend him for aiming high. The problem is that God is an Almighty and jealous God and when one of his own creations begins to place himself at or above God then there will come a judgment on him. One of the purposes of the tribulation is to reveal to the world just how wicked Satan is.

The second reason for the tribulation is to punish those that persecuted God's Children, the Israelites, as well as Christ's bride the Church. *"I will make of thee a great nation. And I will bless thee, and make thy name great; and thou shalt be a blessing. And I will bless them that bless thee, and curse him that curseth thee, and in thee shall all the nations of the World be blessed."* (Genesis 12:2-3). *"For the wrath of God is revealed from heaven against all ungodliness..."*(Romans 1:18). *"And for this cause God shall send them strong delusion, that they should believe a lie. That they all might be damned who believe not the truth."* (2 Thess. 2:11-12). Throughout history we can see how evil people can become, they have persecuted and killed many children of God. As a loving and Holy God, He must punish those who have done evil. Today all sinners have the opportunity to accept Jesus Christ as Savior and avoid the punishment we deserve. There will come a day where God will give the world what it desperately wants, to be in total control, with no Christians whining about sin. In that day there will be no Church, and the world will fall for Satan's lies and for that, this sinful world will receive God's wrath.

The third reason for tribulation is to purge and ultimately redeem Israel. (Zechariah 13:8-9) *"And it shall come to pass, that in all the land 2 parts shall be cut off and die, but the 3rd part shall be left. And I will bring the 3rd part through the fire. And will refine them as silver is refined, and will try them as Gold is tried: they shall call on my name, and I will hear them: I will say, It is my people: and they shall say, The Lord is my God."* (Zecharaiah 13:8-9) *"...Blindness in part is happened to Israel, until the fullness of the Gentiles be come in. And so all Israel shall be saved..."* (Romans 11:25-26).

There are those who say God is done with Israel, that the church of Christ has replaced the nation of Israel as God's chosen people. This is not true. The Bible is clear that Israel is God's chosen people and that one day Israel will return to God, will accept Jesus as their Messiah. Israel's heart is hard though and it will take great tribulation to soften Israel's heart. God will use tribulation to turn Israel's heart to Jesus, Oh what a day that will be!

There is no reference of the Church of Jesus Christ having to go through the tribulation. There is no reason for the Church to endure the tribulation. There are scriptures that seem to suggest that the church will be spared from the tribulation. (1 Thess. 1:9-10) *"...serve the living and true God. And wait for his son in heaven, whom he raised from the dead, even Jesus, which delivered us from the wrath to come."*(1 Thess.1:9-10). *"For God has not appointed us to wrath, but to obtain salvation by our Lord Jesus Christ."* (1 Thess. 5:9). *"Because thou hast kept the word of my patience, I also will keep thee from the hour of temptation which shall come upon all the world, to try them who dwell upon the Earth."* (Rev. 3:10)

Skeptics of the rapture will say that these scriptures simply say that the church will not be sent to Hell, which may be correct, but it seems to be referring to something other than Hell or judgment. I also realize that in its context the Revelation 3:10 passage refers to the church of Sardis and not the entire church; however it may suggest that the church will be spared the tribulation. Add to these scriptures the fact that the book of Revelation stops talking about the church on earth after chapter 4. Could it be the Church is not mentioned on earth because it is not on earth but raptured to be with God in heaven?[24]

There are only 2 passages of scripture that describe the rapture, let's look at these. *"Behold I show you a mystery, we shall not all sleep, but we shall all be changed. In a moment, in the twinkling of an eye, at the last trump. For the trumpet shall sound, and the dead shall be raised incorruptible, and we shall be changed."* (1 Cor. 15:51-52).

"But I would not have you to be ignorant, brethren, concerning them which are asleep, that ye sorrow not, even as others which have no hope. For if we believe that Jesus died and rose again, even so them also which sleep in Jesus will God bring with him...For the Lord himself shall descend from heaven with a shout, with the voice of the arch-angel, and with the trump of God: and the dead in Christ shall rise 1st. Then we which are alive and remain shall be caught up together with them in the clouds, to meet the Lord in the air: and so shall we ever be with the Lord" (1 Thess. 4:13-17).

Paul wrote both of these passages and in both he suggests that this teaching on the rapture is a mystery, but we should not be ignorant about it. Paul also describes those that have died to be asleep. Sleep is the perfect description of what happens to a believer when they die. When a believer dies their bodies are asleep, while their souls are taken to be with Jesus. *"...to be absent from the body is to be present with the Lord."* (2 Cor. 5:8).

When you go to the grave of a loved one who is a Christian you are actually visiting their sleeping body. The essence of who they are, their soul, is alive and well with Jesus Christ. However, one day Jesus and the souls of all Christians will come back to the clouds and there Jesus will shout and the bodies which are asleep will rise up to be reunited with their bodies. If you watch the Walking Dead you may imagine grotesque dead bodies crawling out of the graves. This is not what it will look like, Jesus will transform our old bodies into glorified bodies. These new glorified bodies will reunite with the souls and we will be exactly what God created us to be. Our Souls will have no sin, our bodies will have no flaws...imagine how awesome this will be. As for those who are still alive when Jesus comes to the clouds, they too will be called up, and their bodies will be transformed into glorified bodies and we shall be together with Jesus Christ forever.[25]

One last point needs to be made concerning the rapture. While Christians disagree about the rapture, all Christians anticipate that Jesus will indeed come again. The second coming of Christ is a major tenant of Christian faith. If you study all the scriptures that refer to Christ coming again, you can't help but notice the differing descriptions of that second coming. Some critics simply chalk it up to the fact that the Bible always contradicts itself, however if you believe every word of the Bible is true then how do you explain what seems to be contradictions in scripture when it comes to describing Jesus' 2nd coming? In the scripture's we have just studied (1 Cor 15:51-52) and (1 Thess. 4:13-17) It describes Jesus coming quickly in the clouds of the air with a shout and with angels blowing trumpets and with the dead rising from their graves to be with Jesus in the clouds.

Let's compare this with a couple of other verses. *"Behold, the day of the Lord cometh...I will gather all nations against Jerusalem to battle...then shall the Lord go forth and fight against those nations...and his feet shall stand in that day upon the mount of Olives,...and ½ of the mountain shall remove...The Lord my God shall come and all the saints with thee."* (Zecharaiah 14:1-5). *"And I saw heaven opened, and behold a white horse, and he that sat upon him was called Faithfull and true...His eyes were as the flame of fire, and on his head were many crowns...and his name is called The Word of God. And the armies which were in heaven followed him upon white horses...Out of his mouth goeth a sharp sword, that with it he should smite the nations."* (Rev. 19:11-15).

In these passages it speaks of Jesus coming out of heaven riding a white horse holding a sharp sword accompanied by an army from heaven. It describes a great army formed by all the nations coming against Jerusalem and Jesus coming down from heaven and defeating them. It goes on to say that Jesus will set his feet on the Mt of Olives. This seems to be describing a separate event than what (1 Cor.15:51-52) and (1 Thess. 4:13-17) describe.

At the rapture Jesus never sets his foot on earth, there are no armies gathered, there are no horses. There are graves being opened and dead bodies rising in the clouds...this is a much different scene. So there are 3 ways to explain this. 1. This is another contradiction in the Bible.

2. Maybe somehow the 2 stories will make sense once it takes place, perhaps Jesus will meet the saints in the clouds as the dead rise to meet him, then everyone will hop on white horses and battle the armies that quickly gathered, then Jesus will set foot on the Mt. of Olives.

3. Jesus will 1st rapture up his church, the tribulation will take place, Satan will gather the nations against Israel, Israel having their eyes opened during the tribulation will cry out to God, Jesus will hear their cries and saddle up his White Horse and His bride the church will follow and with a shout Jesus will defeat the nations, Israel will accept Jesus as Messiah and be redeemed. [25]

I believe when you consider all the verses relating to the end times that Jesus will rapture the church up before the tribulation. Of course this is my opinion which certainly could be wrong. As always I suggest you should study God's Word for yourself and let the Holy Spirit guide you.

No one knows for sure how the events of the end times will unfold. What is certain is that Jesus will return! People often wonder if they are truly saved. One litmus test is to honestly ask yourself how would you feel if Jesus were to return today? If that thought excites you then you are probably saved, if that thought scares you in any way then you may want to ask Jesus to come into your heart and make your salvation sure. Are you ready?

The Bible is Spiritually Sound

"I am the way, the truth, and the life; no one comes to the Father but by me." **(John 14:6)**

The heart of the Bible is its spiritual truth. While I believe it is important to understand that the Bible is historically proven, scientifically reliable and prophetically accurate, it is the gospel message that must be understood and retold to a world that desperately needs to hear it. The Bible was given to us to allow the world to understand the reality of our sinful condition, and God's loving plan to redeem mankind from it. There are five spiritual truths taught in the Bible that will help to find life's true meaning: 1. We are created in the image of God, 2. Man is sinful by nature, 3. God loves sinners and sent His Son to pay our sin debt, 4. We must place our faith in Jesus Christ, and 5. Once saved, we must live a life of love.[1]

We are created in the image of God. *"So God created man in his own image, in the image of God created he him; male and female he created he them. And God blessed them..."* (Gen. 1:27-28).

The most basic spiritual truth in the Bible is that we are created by a loving God in his image. One question many ask is, "Why did God create man in the first place?" One of the obvious reasons could have been was that God was lonely and needed to have a relationship with someone. This may sound logical but the Bible says otherwise. *"The Lord possessed me in the beginning of his way, before his works of old...when he prepared the heavens, I was there...when he appointed the foundations of the Earth: then I was by him, as one brought up with him: and I was daily his delight, rejoicing always before him."* (Proverbs 8:22-30).

149

The Bible is Spiritually Sound.

The Bible clearly teaches that God is a trinity which enables him to delight in himself. God is not in need of anyone or anything else. So then the question remains, "Why did God create man?" Paul explains why we were created here: *"But God, who is rich in mercy, for his great love wherewith he loved us, even when we were dead in sins, hath quickened us together in heavenly places in Christ Jesus. That in the ages to come he might show the exceeding riches of his grace in his kindness toward us through Christ Jesus."* (Ephesians 2:4-7).

Everything God has done, his creation, his plan for our redemption, his amazing grace and abiding love all demonstrate the need for God to be glorified. John explains this here: *"Thou art worthy, oh Lord, to receive glory and honor and power: for thou hast created all things, and for thy pleasure they are and were created."* (Rev.4:11).

The Bible tells us that the entire universe was created by God for his pleasure. Each one of us were created to uniquely bring glory to God. Some bring glory to God by preaching his word, some by singing praises to him, some bring glory to God by encouraging others, and some do so through nursing, teaching, or cooking. In fact, we can bring glory to God within any occupation.

This concept has transformed the way I work. I no longer dread going to work, I go to work looking for opportunities to encourage others, hoping this encouragement will draw my co-workers to Christ. The negative attitudes so many people display toward work amaze me. I have noticed that if you work with people who project negative attitudes, it is so easy to share their attitude. The best way to break the cycle of long negative days, when you may feel like you need a strong cold drink to get through another day, is to begin your day in God's word and in prayer. When you begin your day focused on God, you cannot help but have a strong desire to bring God glory, the very thing the Bible says we were created for.

Our society is so focused on pleasing ourselves that we may give little or no thought to others or to God. It is no surprise that many have turned to drugs, alcohol, and pornography in an effort to satisfy their own selfish desire. The truth is that while the world is full of things that will bring temporary pleasure, there is nothing in this world that will bring the lasting joy that comes from glorifying God. Just stop and think about it, who would know better about what will bring contentment and lasting Joy than the one who created you, and loves you?

Often we ignore or reject God's word and lean to our own understanding. This may bring pleasure for a while but always ends in emptiness, and often results in dependence on something harmful to us. The problem is that any of these things will ultimately control our lives, leaving us empty.

Society portrays materialism as the vehicle that will bring us fulfillment, but this is simply untrue. If it were true, Hollywood would be the happiest, most content city in the world. Instead it is comprised of some of the most perverse, insecure, and unhappy people on Earth. Take a look into the lives of the world's most famous and successful people of Hollywood: Elvis Presley, Michael Jackson, Whitney Houston, Heath Ledger, Robin Williams, Kirk Corban, Jimi Hendrix, the list goes on. The flip side of this list is those who bring glory to God.

The most joy filled people I know are those who demonstrate love to others and to God. They may not be wealthy, they are certainly not famous, but they truly enjoy life. If you want true joy and contentment, if you want to find deep purpose in the smallest things, look for ways to bring glory to God and you will find peace and joy. This does not mean that you will suddenly be tiptoeing through the tulips, but you will find the only thing capable of filling the hole in your heart, the one you keep trying to fill with the things of this world. You were created to bring God glory.

The Bible has explained why God created the universe, to bring him glory. Now let us look at how the understanding that you were created by a loving God answers five of humanity's most basic questions: 1. Where did we come from?, 2. Who we are?, 3. Why we are here?, 4. How we should live?, and 5. Where we are going?[2]

Where did we come from? *"For thou hast possessed my reins: thou hast covered me in my mother's womb. I will praise thee; for I am fearfully and wonderfully made: marvelous are thy works; and that my soul knoweth right well."* (Psalm 139:13-14).

The great difference that comes from understanding that you were created in the image of a loving God and believing the falsehood children may be taught in school (that they simply evolved over millions of years) cannot be emphasized enough. If it were true that we are nothing more than a link in some evolutionary chain, then life would be truly without purpose or meaning. Darwin taught that only the strong survive, that life is ultimately about natural selection. Which traits are strong? Which are weak? The strong traits remain while the weak traits simply become extinct.

Hitler became an evolutionary hero when he put Darwin's theory to the test, attempting to assist evolution by establishing a super race of people, exterminating what he perceived as weaker races. What a great hero! Why is this not the narrative? Why does society correctly view Hitler as a monster? Could it be that humans are created in the image of a loving God and are much more than a link in an evolutionary chain? What is it that gives human life importance? The simple answer is that humans are important because we were created in our loving God's image. We have value in that we are all part of God's plan. This is why Hitler is a monster not a hero and this is why slavery is wrong.

If natural selection were true, what would be wrong with slavery? If one race was superior to another race and subjected a weaker race to work for free, that would illustrate what evolution is all about, simply a part of natural selection. We know instinctively that slavery is wrong because we were all created in God's image. No race is superior to any other, in fact we are all from one race of sinners. Human life is of great value to God therefore it should be of great value to society as well.

Who are we? What is our identity? *"When we were children, we were in bondage under the elements of the world. But when the fullness of time was come, God sent forth his son, made of a woman, made under the law to redeem them that were under the law, that we might receive the adoption of sons, and because ye are sons, God hath sent forth the spirit of his son into your hearts, crying Abba father. Wherefore thou art no more a servant, but a son, and if a son, then an heir of God through Christ."* (Galatians 4:3-7).

When we are born we are identified as God's most wonderful creation, created in His very image to serve Him and bring Him glory. This gives everyone born great value. In fact we are so valuable to God that He sent His only begotten son to die on the cross to pay the sin debt only He could pay. Those who accept Jesus Christ as Lord and Savior are no longer simply God's servants but children of God.

As children of God we have the amazing privilege to go to the almighty creator God and call him daddy...Wow! We are given a wonderful identity as a child of God. What a stark difference! The Bible says we are made children of God through Jesus Christ, while our kids may be taught that they descended from apes. Knowing your true identity makes an enormous difference in how you live your life. If you believe you descended from an ape, you have no real identity. So many today spend their entire lives trying to find something or someone to identify with.

Some are identified by their sexual orientation, others are identified by their political ideals, still others like myself are identified by their favorite sports teams. (Roll Tide!) These labels can give some identities which often end up defining a persons life.

 The sad thing is the world can offer you no lasting identity. This is because the world has rejected the only person who can give you a lasting identity and that person is Jesus Christ. Matthew West sings a great song, "Hello My Name Is", which describes how this feels in the chorus: *"Hello my name is child of the one true king. I have been saved. I have been changed. I have been set free. 'Amazing Grace' is the song I sing. I am no longer defined by the wreckage behind. I am a child of the one true king!"* [3] What a wonderful feeling to come from being a sinner, a failure, and a disappointment to being transformed by the blood of Jesus Christ into a child of our creator, God.

If you understand that not only were you created in God's image, but that Jesus shed His blood so that you could be called

154

a child of God, that means your life has great purpose and you have the wonderful privilege of a personal relationship with the creator of the universe. I am the father of four children, and nothing brings me more joy than when my children sit on my lap and want to simply be with their daddy. This is exactly how our Father God feels when we come to him in prayer, when we worship him, when we read his word; when we do these things we form a lasting relationship with our heavenly Father that will last for eternity. How do you want to be identified?

The truth is you are not some distant descendant of apes, instead you were created by a loving God who made a way through his son for you to be called a child of the Most High King. Have you identified yourself as a child of God through Jesus Christ?

Why are we here? What is the purpose of life? *"Let us hear the conclusion of the whole matter: fear God, and keep his commandments; for this is the whole duty of man."* (Ecc.12:13). This was written at the end of King Solomon's life. He had the unique opportunity to search the world for meaning and so he did. He was the son of King David and was given great wisdom from God.

He began by pursuing pleasure, so he gave himself up to wine and a life of partying, but found that it did not satisfy him and brought no meaning to life. Next he pursued hard work. He built houses and planted vineyards, but that brought no lasting satisfaction. He tried accumulating great wealth as he collected silver, gold, and priceless treasures from other kings, but this too brought him no satisfaction. Next he turned to education and he studied all the world's philosophies but all of this knowledge brought him no meaning or purpose.

The Bible is Spiritually Sound.

He soon became depressed at all the meaningless in life until finally at the end of his life Solomon found the only thing to ever bring meaning and purpose to his life was to fear God and keep his commandments. This may sound ridiculous, but remember God is our creator, Is it not logical that obeying Him would bring us contentment, purpose, and meaning? It is no wonder that much of the world today is hurting. We have not only stopped obeying God, we have openly rejected God by removing his word from the very schools that were founded and based on that same Word. The truth is that no amount of funding or testing will improve our schools; only if we return the Bible as the foundation of education will our schools once again lead the world.

The world is looking everywhere to find meaning and joy. Listen to what the apostle John says, *"Herein is my Father glorified, that ye bare much fruit..."* (John 15:8) Our joy is directly related by the glory we bring God. Understand that joy is different from happiness. Joy, unlike happiness, does not depend on your circumstances. Your happiness changes as your circumstances change. For example, if you win the lottery you will no doubt be happy, but if your house burns down you will be unhappy. Joy remains despite your circumstances. This is how you explain Paul and Silas singing from a jail cell because they had joy in spite of their unfortunate circumstances. The joy all Christians should have comes from understanding the reason we are all here, to bring glory to God.[4]

How should we live? Where does morality come from? *"If a man say, I love God, and hateth his brother, he is a liar; for he that loveth not his brother whom he hath seen, how can he love God whom he hath not seen? And this commandment have we from him. That he who loveth God love his brother also."* (1 John

The Bible is Spiritually Sound.

4:20-21). One question that puzzles some evolutionists is, 'Where did morality come from?" If natural selection determines how traits are passed down, it would seem that most morals would hinder this natural process. Why would every single civilization on Earth have a similar set of moral codes to live by if our lives are simply an evolutionary phase? Would it not seem natural for stronger people to overpower weaker people? Why would it matter if the strongest person steals from someone weaker, or subjugates someone weaker, or even kills someone weaker? If we are merely a part of some evolutionary chain it would not matter at all. The fact is that morality does matter a great deal, and the fact that morality matters points directly to a loving creator. The Bible includes many laws, the Ten Commandments viewed as the major ones. These Ten Commandments are certainly not unique to Christianity or even Judaism. The basic laws of morality are universal. You should not lie, steal, or kill. You should obey your parents and treat each other with respect. All successful civilizations adhere to these basic moral laws.

Our society has become so apathetic that many people have no strong opinion when it comes to questions of morality. There appears to be a belief that there is no real moral truth and that morals should not be legislated or taught in schools.

Frank Turek and Norman Geisler ask some insightful questions in their book, "I Don't Have Enough Faith to be an Atheist". Did it matter that the U.S. Supreme Court ruled that blacks were not citizens but property of the slave owners? Or that Nazi's believed that the Jewish race was weaker than the Aryan race? Does it matter that our children are taught that they evolved from apes? Or that an unborn baby is simply a choice and is not a living person? Clearly morality does matter, and when it is

157

taught and legislated it makes an enormous difference. This points to the fact that a moral God created us.[5]

What is our destiny? What happens when we die? *"Let not your heart be troubled: ye believe in God, believe also in me. In my Father's house are many mansions: if it were not so, I would have told you. I go to prepare a place for you. And if I go and prepare a place for you, I will come again, and receive you unto myself; that where I am, there ye may be also."* (John 14:1-3). Jesus tells us here that those that believe in him should not worry, because he is preparing a place for us to be with him when we die. He promises us that where he is, there we will be also. This is what gives Christians hope. This hope is not like the hope we often talk about, where you might hope to win the lottery.

The hope we have in Christ is one of certainty. It consists more of looking forward to something, rather than wishing something might happen. As Christians our hope, our destiny, our eternity rests in Jesus Christ. This certainty is not based on my ability as a Christian to follow Christ, if so then my hope is only as good as I am, which is not too good. This certainty is based on the ability of Jesus to forgive my sins. The Bible says that the blood of Christ washes away all of my sin. This includes all of my sin in the past, present, and future. I know that I am going to heaven not because I believe I deserve to, but because Jesus promises that I will be with him if I believe in him.

This belief enables us to live differently than others who have no hope. When you are certain you are going to heaven to live eternally with Jesus, it gives you courage and peace that nothing else can provide. The world without this certainty is spiritually unstable, as people continue to search for purpose in what often seems meaningless. When tragedy strikes it often paralyzes people in fear. Satan uses this fear to control man's behavior. Jesus has come to remove all fear and oh, how wonderful this is! I love how Paul describes this in Romans, Chapter 8: *"If God be for us, who can be against us? Who shall separate us from the love of Christ? Shall tribulation, or distress, or persecution, or famine, or nakedness, or peril, or sword? Nay, in all these things we are more than conquerors through Him that loved us."* (Romans 8:31)

This helps us to face this life with no fear. Fear keeps us from doing many things that God deigned that we do. Our faith in Christ removes this fear so that the more faithful we are to Christ, the less fear of the world we have. Knowing our eternal future should help us become courageous. There are thousands of examples of how this wonderful hope in Christ has enabled Christians to withstand severe persecution, tragedy, and great suffering with a loving, forgiving, and courageous spirit. I love it! We are more than conquerors through Christ! Unfortunately many Christians, myself included, do not exhibit this type of faith and this causes the world to wonder if Christianity is real. I believe when Christians begin to truly act on our faith, and become more than conquerors, the world begins to follow our example.

Man is sinful by nature. *"For all have sinned, and come short of the glory of God."* (Romans 3:23).

The fall of man into sin is one of the most basic spiritual concepts in the Bible. There is great division among the world's religions concerning the basic nature of man. In fact, there is great division among Christians as to the basic nature of man. As the father of four children, I never had to teach any of them

159

how to behave selfishly. I did have to teach them how to share, how to be polite, how to be considerate of others. This indicates man's sinful nature. Do not misunderstand. I am not saying my kids are bad, I'm saying they are sinful. One of today's major problems is the perception that we are all basically good and that as long as we have a little religion, do a few good deeds, maybe support a few charities or give to a needy family at Christmas, that God will approve and let us into heaven. This mistaken theology will send more people to Hell than all the atheistic teachings about evolution, or the liberals' insistence that Christians should have no voice in government or all the trash Hollywood churns out to our theaters.

There is no greater threat to the souls in America today than the belief that we are all good enough, and do not need any relationship with God. This is directly opposite to what the Bible teaches about the basic nature of man: man is sinful by nature. In this chapter we will look at the Biblical definition of sin, man's fall into sin, and how Adam's original sin affected the world. Finally we will also answer a question that many have pondered: why did God allow man to sin in the first place?

What is sin? *"But he that sinneth against me wrongeth his own soul: all they that hate me love death."* (Proverbs 8:36). The Hebrew word for sin is khata, which means "to miss the mark". We sin when we miss the mark of God's righteousness, sinning against the holiness of God. So sin is not simply a mistake, it is actually rebellion against God. Following are two quotes that define sin. *"Sin may be defined ultimately as anything in the creature which does not express, or which is contrary to the Holy character of the Creator."* James Oliver Buswell Jr. *"Sin is any lack of conformity, active or passive, to the moral law of God.*

The Bible is Spiritually Sound.

Sin is failure to live up to what God expects of us in act, thought, and being." Millard Erickson[6]

Man's original sin teaches us a lot about man's sinful nature, Satan's subtle temptations, and man's instinctive reaction to sin. Man's original sin also causes us to ask why God allowed man to sin in the first place.

"And the Lord God commanded the man, saying, of every tree of the garden thou mayest freely eat. But of the tree of the knowledge of good and evil, thou shalt not eat of it: for in the day that thou eatest thereof thou shalt surely die." (Genesis 2:16-17). Why did God place such a stipulation on Adam if He foreknew Adam would eat the forbidden fruit? This is a question every student of the Bible has contemplated. Let me begin by saying no one truly understands the mind of God. *"Oh the depth of his riches both of the wisdom and knowledge of God! How unsearchable are his judgments, and his ways past finding out. For who hath known the mind of the Lord?"* (Romans 11:33-34).

The Bible is full of mysteries that no one truly knows the answer to. This has caused many to doubt the validity of the Bible. This line of reasoning amazes me. If God is our creator, as His creation would you expect us to know all of the reasons for God's actions? It seems to me that the fact the Bible is full of things that are impossible to fully understand demonstrates how authentic the Bible truly is. As to why God allowed Adam to sin in the Garden of Eden, no one knows the full answer, but here are a couple of ideas as to why God allowed man to sin. *"Even when we were dead in sins, hath quickened us together with Christ, (by grace ye are saved ;) That in the ages to come he might shew the exceeding riches of his grace in his kindness toward us through Christ Jesus."* (Ephesians 2:5+7).

Ultimately God allowed Adam to sin so that God could demonstrate the richness of his loving grace by redeeming man's sin through His son Jesus Christ. It is often hard to see the big picture of God's ultimate plan when we are here on Earth suffering with the effects of sin.

Many have a hard time accepting how a loving God could entrap his creation. Many believe that God caused man to sin by placing the forbidden tree in the Garden of Eden in the first place. The truth is God did not cause man to sin, he simply knew that he would sin. Here is an example of how this works. If I were to place a pack of Reese's Peanut Butter Cups, a bottle of my wife's perfume, and a cell phone on the kitchen table and tell my kids not to touch anything on the table, I could tell you exactly what would happen. My oldest twin Jonathan would eat the Reese's Peanut Butter Cups, my daughter Kathryn would put on too much of my wife's perfume, my teenage son Logan would use all the data on the cell phone, and my younger twin Nathan would tell me play by play how it all happened.

Did I force my kids to do these things? No, but I know my children well enough to predict their actions. So, while God certainly knew that Adam would eat the forbidden fruit, he did not force Adam to sin. Adam freely chose to sin. It is this free will of man that is very important to God. Certainly God could have created man to be subservient to Him. He could make us live Holy lives, but there is no love in this. It is God's plan to have his creation freely choose to follow Him out of love. I do not claim to fully understand this, but do not ever forget this

The Bible is Spiritually Sound.

wonderful truth, *"And we know that all things work together for good to them that love God."* (Romans 8:28).

 While I may not know exactly why God allowed Adam to sin I know for certain that God was not being unfair or cruel. He was putting into motion a wonderful love story that ends with sinful man living eternally in heaven with a Holy loving God.

God gave Adam clear and concise instructions that he could eat of anything in the Garden of Eden except from the Tree of the Knowledge of good and evil. God's word is always clear and concise. It is so simple that my nine year old daughter understands it well enough to know that she needs a relationship with Jesus Christ, who paid the price for her sins.

The problem is not that God has failed to give us the truth of his word, it is that we are guilty of ignoring or even changing God's word. Notice how the Bible describes the fall of man. *"Now the serpent was more subtle than any beast of the field which the Lord God had made. And he said unto the woman, Yea, hath God said, ye shall not eat of every tree of the garden."* (Genesis 3:1)

 Satan came to Eve and questioned the Word of God. This led to doubt. Satan continues to do this today. How many cast doubt on many clear teachings of God's Word? People today question whether Hell is real, whether homosexuality is a sin, and whether or not the church ought to be evangelistic. These are all clearly taught in God's Word and there should be no doubt. When we begin to question God's Word we doubt its plain truth. This leads to confusion as to what truth really is. Is there any doubt that Satan has cast doubt on God's Word? Few today view the Bible as being true, which has led to the fact that all philosophies are treated in the same way as the Word of God.

"...God hath said, ye shall not eat of it, neither shall ye touch it, lest ye die. And the Serpent said unto the woman, ye shall not surely die." (Genesis 3:3-4)

Satan not only casts doubt on God's Word, he outright denies and changes God's word. He suggests to Eve that God would never allow you to die. This sounds a lot like the argument that a loving God would never send anyone to Hell. Satan is an expert on casting doubt and eventually refuting God's Word. This is why God has given us His Word in writing, so that we can know the truth and reject all the doubt and confusion Satan tries to cast onto God's Word. The Bible is the only source of absolute truth in the world and anyone who doubts it or changes it in any way is no doubt being influenced by the lies of Satan, which began in the Garden of Eden.

"For God doth know that in the day ye eat thereof, then your eyes shall be opened, and ye shall be as gods, knowing good and evil." (Genesis 3:5) Satan not only denies God's word, he suggests that God is trying to keep you from having your eyes opened. Satan suggests that man can become a god, and this idea continues to be popular among religions and cults today. The idea that we can become a god is one of Satan's most coveted lies. So many today are not interested in growing close to God; instead they would rather become a god. Man is so full of pride that many find this idea appealing.

Satan often appeals to man's pride because it is certainly a weakness that we all share. Man cannot become like a god. We are all sinners who deserve death but have been given a wonderful opportunity to become a child of God. The idea that we can become a god is a lie from Satan himself. Satan knows this to be true and does all he can to lead people away from

God's wonderful truth. Satan uses the same tactics today that he used in the Garden of Eden, tricks that have been proven to be extremely effective over the years. It would be wise to take note of Satan's tendencies: to cast doubt on God's Word, and then to ultimately deny and replace God's Word. The best way to guard yourself against Satan's deceptions is by keeping the Word of God close to your heart.

"And when the woman saw that the tree was good for food, and that it was pleasant to the eyes, and a tree to be desired to make one wise, she took of the fruit thereof, and did eat, and gave also unto her husband with her; and he did eat." (Genesis 3:6) It is easy to simply blame Satan for tempting us. As a child I would often get in trouble and would say, *"The Devil made me do it."* This may be true, but it does not change the fact that I chose to sin. We see in the very first account of man sinning some important truths. God gives us a clear and concise word. Satan casts doubt on God's word and ultimately changes God's word into a lie. We then choose to sin against God. While some may blame God for allowing man to sin and others blame Satan for tempting man to sin, the ultimate reason that we sin is that we choose to do so. We can blame our sin on no one except ourselves.

Note the three specific areas that tempted Eve. She perceived that the tree was good for food, depicting the lust of the flesh. We desire to meet our basic physical needs and will do almost anything to satisfy these needs. This frequently includes addiction to food, to alcohol, or to drugs, all of which have absolutely destroyed many lives. Next Eve noted that the forbidden fruit was pleasant to the eyes. Our society is obsessed with physical beauty. The internet has become the world's greatest vehicle to promote an ever growing narcissistic society.

Pornography has developed into one of the most lucrative businesses, even as it causes so many to fall into unhealthy relationships.

Finally, Eve desired the wisdom that would come from eating the forbidden fruit. This depicts the most common temptation for the more sophisticated, religious and educated among us, the pride of life. Our society prides itself on the growing amount of knowledge we possess. We have become so educated that many no longer feel a need for God. This pride will unwittingly lead many away from God and into Hell. Sins of the flesh like drugs or pornography feel wrong but the sin of pride often feels good, as if nothing is amiss. This is such a dangerous idea that I believe that pride will lead more to Hell than sins of the flesh.

Satan used these same 3 temptations on Jesus as he tempted him after forty days in the desert. He began by tempting Jesus to turn the stones to bread, which tempted Jesus' flesh at a time he was extremely hungry. Next, Satan tempted Jesus by taking him to the top of the mountain and offering him all he could see, tempting him with his sight. Finally, Satan tempted Jesus with his pride as he asked Jesus to jump off a cliff and allow angels to come minister to him, which would reveal his glory. Jesus overcame each of these temptations by using God's word. This is no accident my friend; the Bible is the best defense against Satan's temptations.

"And they heard the voice of the Lord God...and Adam and his wife hid themselves from the presence of the Lord God." (Genesis 3:8) This is the key to why sin is so toxic to all of mankind. Our sin results in us running and hiding from God. It is this separation from God that causes depression, fear, and anxiety. This separation from God also causes us to sin even

more, which makes us run further from God to hide. It is not long until we have run so far from God that we are no longer praying, reading the Bible, or going to church.

This is why repentance is such an important part of Christian life. In fact, it is this repentant heart that caused God to call King David a man after his own heart. Have you ever wondered why a man who committed adultery and murder could be considered a man after God's own heart? The answer is that David was always quick to confess his sin and get forgiveness. This is the secret to a joy filled Christian life. It is not that we never sin; it is rather that we quickly admit our sin to God instead of running and hiding from Him.

The truth is every one of us struggles with sin. God knows this, so why try to hide our sin from an all knowing God? Christians who try to appear if they no longer struggle with sin are living a lie. When we sin, we must not run and hide from God. We need to run to God and fall on our knees and beg for forgiveness. The Apostle John put it this way, *"If we say that we have no sin, we deceive ourselves, and the truth is not in us. If we confess our sins, he is faithful and just to forgive us our sins, and to cleanse us from all unrighteousness."* (1 John 1:8-9)

What an awesome, loving God who understands our weakness, loves sinners, and is faithful to forgive our sins each and every time we confess our sin to him. Why would we run and hide from such a forgiving and loving God? We need to be more like King David, a sinner who was honest with God and with himself. If you have been running from God, afraid of what He may do, and ashamed of your sinful behavior, may I challenge you to stop running and return to a loving God who is waiting to forgive you.

"And the Lord God called unto Adam, and said unto him, where art thou? (Genesis 3:9) Here we see how great God's desire is to have a relationship with his greatest creation. Adam and Eve had openly rebelled against God's Word and yet God called out to them. What a picture of God's loving and graceful heart as He calls out to Adam and Eve as they try to hide their sin from God. God chases us down not to punish us, but to wrap his loving arms around us and forgive us. He knows we are sinners, but He still loves us and wants desperately to have a relationship with each one of us.

We need to examine the devastating results of man's sin. First we will see how sin effected Satan. *"And the Lord God said unto the serpent, Because thou hast done this, thou art cursed above all cattle, and above every beast of the field; upon thy belly shalt thou go, and dust shalt thou eat all the days of thy life: And I will put enmity between thee and the woman, and between thy seed and her seed; it shall bruise thy head, and thou shalt bruise his heel."* (Genesis 3:14-15)

Many liberal Bible scholars say this is a way to explain how men hate and fear snakes, and that snakes are cursed to crawl on their bellies. While this curse does include snakes crawling, it goes much further than that. In fact this verse is known as the *"Proto-Evangel"* or the 1st gospel. Here we see God's plan to defeat Satan and redeem man. I like how Harold Wilmington translates this, *"And there will be intense hatred between Satan and Christ. Eventually, Christ will crush the head of Satan, while suffering a heel wound in the process"*[6]. God planned for Jesus to die on the cross, which is analogous to bumping his heel, while crushing Satan's head, ending Satan's hold on mankind and freeing man from the penalty of sin.

The Bible is Spiritually Sound.

How did sin affect Eve? *"Unto the woman he said, I will greatly multiply thy sorrow and thy conception; in sorrow thou shalt bring forth children; and thy desire shall be to thy husband, and he shall rule over thee."*(Genesis 3:16)

Very few preachers dare to preach from this verse these days. Many would say this verse is outdated, but it is really important to understand what God is saying, as well as what He is not saying.

First of all, God has given women birth pains which represent a couple of things. These pains exemplify the Christian life which is full of suffering but will one day yield a new glorified body for those in Christ. It also represents the last days which will be full of war, storms and death, but will transform this old sinful Earth into a new glorified Earth. This reveals how suffering can be a blessing when you understand that only through suffering can God bless his children. Remember this is not God's original plan. God created a perfect world and placed Adam and Eve there and when they chose to sin, it brought pain and suffering to new life.[6]

The Bible includes some very difficult verses, the following quote is one of them. However unpopular it might be, it is still true. Women were created to come beside and help man, not to be man's servant. According to the Bible the husband is the spiritual leader of the family. *"Wives, submit yourselves unto your own husbands, as unto the Lord. For the husband is the head of the wife, even as Christ is the head of the church...Husbands love your wives, even as Christ also loved the church, and gave himself for it."* (Ephesians 5:22-25).

Marriage was established by God partly to portray how Jesus loves the church. While many today are offended by the fact that wives should submit to their husbands, you must understand the role of husbands. A husband should love his wife and be willing to sacrifice himself for her. When a husband loves his wife in this way, his wife will have no problem submitting to him.

The Bible in no way advocates for husbands to rule over their wives as though they are inferior. Wives are not inferior to husbands but are equal to them. Together they form a family wherein each serves the family as both the husband and the wife submit to one another. The family is more joyful when the husband leads the family in worship, as this is how God designed marriage. This does not say that if the husband fails to lead the family to worship that the wife cannot. If the husband neglects his role in the family, which happens quite often, then the wife should lead her children to worship God.

There are many cases where the children actually lead their parents to worship God. While these are not ideal, they are still preferable to having no one in the family worshiping God. The bottom line is that God established the family as one unit where everyone in that unit must submit to one another. This helps us as prideful sinners to learn how to put others' needs above our own, becoming more like Jesus Christ.

We also need to examine how sin affected Adam. *"And unto Adam he said...cursed is the ground for thy sake; in sorrow shalt thou eat of it all the days of thy life...In the sweat of thy face shalt thou eat bread, till thou return unto the ground...for dust thou art, and unto dust shalt thou return."* (Genesis 3:17-19)

God made man's work laborious. In the Garden of Eden food was produced with no effort by man, but now man must work hard and toil the land in order to produce food. All this hard work, this blood, sweat and tears will produce food and shelter, but this work will not bring salvation. Adam would eventually die and return to the dust from where he came. Here we see the great cost of man's sin: death. God had warned Adam and Eve that if they ate of forbidden fruit, it would result in death. Two types of death were a result of man's sin: a physical death which happens to all creation, and spiritual death, also referred to as the second death. *"Even when we were dead in sins, hath quickened us together with Christ."*(Ephesians 2:5)

Sin's curse affects all mankind, as we are all born into sin. The Bible describes us as dead in sin. Those who have not accepted Jesus Christ as savior are spiritually dead, as sin has separated them from God. Much like cut flowers which appear to be full of life as they sit in a vase, they are actually dead. They have been separated from their roots and will soon lose their beautiful petals to wilt and die. We are born into sin and while we may seem to be full of life, we will die unless we are born again and given eternal life through the blood of Jesus Christ. Jesus has made a way for us to be brought back into a loving relationship with God.

We can also see how Adam's sin affected the Earth. *"Cursed is the ground for thy sake...Thorns also and thistles shall it bring forth to thee."* (Genesis 3:17-18) Many wonder why God created a world full of storms, volcanoes, earthquakes, and other natural disasters. The truth is that God created a perfect world and placed man it. When man sinned, God cursed the Earth, bringing death to the Earth. Before man sinned there was no death on Earth, no storms, earthquakes or volcanoes. None of these were created by God. They are the result of man's sin.

This is why I believe in a young Earth and reject evolution. There are those who accept evolution but believe that God used evolution to create what we see today. The problem with this is that God would be the ultimate cause of death and pain, not man's sin. The Bible is clear that the Garden of Eden was God's perfect creation until man sinned, causing God to curse the Earth. If God allowed death before Adam's sin, there would be a huge theological problem. God would be the source of death, which would make him a cruel and unloving God.

The Bible teaches that through the sin of one man, death came to Earth and that with the death of one perfect man, all sin was paid. *"For since by man came death, by man came also the resurrection of the dead. For as in Adam all die, even so in Christ shall all be made alive."* (1 Corinthians 15:21-22) Death is the result of one man's sin. Through the resurrection of one man, Jesus Christ, all men will be made alive. If evolution were true it would mean that death would have come prior to man's sin. This would negate the possibility of one man providing life for all.

The truth is that God created the entire universe in six literal days, just as Adam and Eve were created fully grown and were not born as into the world as babies. God created a fully formed Earth, moon, and sun in 6 days. When Adam chose to sin, this sin cursed the Earth, which introduced pain, suffering, and ultimately death into God's perfect creation. This is the answer to one of skeptics' most often asked questions, "Why does God allow suffering?" God did not create the world to include pain, suffering or death.

It was man's sin that brought suffering to this world. God does gracefully provide forgiveness for man's sin and eternal redemption through the blood of his son Jesus Christ.

Finally we can examine how man's sin affected God. *"And on the 7th day God ended his work which he had made; and He rested."* (Genesis 2:2) After God created the universe and all the life on Earth, He rested. This rest did not last long, however. When Adam sinned it caused God to get up from his rest and begin a much more difficult work than creating the universe. He began to work on redeeming man from sin and restoring a loving relationship with man. *But Jesus answered them, My Father worketh hitherto, and I work."* (John 5:17)

God began work by searching for Adam and Eve in the Garden of Eden, where they were hiding. Throughout the Bible we find God searching for sinful men. *"After these things the word of the Lord came unto Abram in a vision, saying Fear not Abram, I am thy shield, and thy exceeding great reward"* (Genesis 15: 1).

"And God spake unto Moses and said unto him, I am the Lord. And I appeared unto Abraham, unto Isaac, and unto Jacob...and I have also established my covenant with them to give them the Land of Canaan...And I have also heard the groaning of the children of Israel, whom the Egyptians keep in bondage." (Genesis 6:2-5).

"And the Lord said unto Joshua, This day will I begin to magnify thee in the sight of all Israel...as I was with Moses, so I will be with thee." (Joshua 3:7).

"Now God had brought Daniel into favour and tender love with the prince of the eunuchs." (Daniel1:9).

The Bible is Spiritually Sound.

Throughout the Old Testament God was actively working on behalf of those who placed their trust in Him. In the New Testament God sent his Son to continue this work. *"For the Son of man is come to seek and to save the lost."* (Luke 19:10). The Bible describes God as the one who searches for believers-- what a picture of God's love! God pursues a relationship with each of us despite the fact that we reject his love to please our own selfish desires instead.

God not only became active in the lives of those who placed their faith in God, He sent his son to save man from sin. *"For God so loved the world that He gave his only begotten Son, that whosoever believeth in him should not perish, but have everlasting life. For God sent not His Son into the world to condemn the world; but that the world through him might be saved."* (John 3:16-17). God's work in creating the entire universe and all the life on Earth required only a few words over the span of 6 days. God's work to redeem mankind from sin required that God send His Son to Earth and shed his blood on the cross. Man's sin was extremely costly to God, yet God loved us so much that He sent His Son to pay the sin debt no one else could pay.

Adam's original sin still affects us today. *"Wherefore, as by one man sin entered into the world, and death by sin; and so death passed upon all men, for that all have sinned."* *"For as by one man's disobedience many were made sinners, so by the obedience of one shall many be made righteous."* (Romans 5:12 + 19)

The Bible clearly teaches us that we are all sinners. The truth is that we choose to sin because we descended from Adam. We are sinners; sin defines our very nature. As little children we are selfish, and as I said earlier, no one has to teach a child to be selfish. This points to the sinful nature that was passed down from Adam. Adam's sin had even greater effect on all of mankind. Following is an abbreviated list of the consequences of Adam's sin. Sin brought fear, *"I heard thy voice in the garden, and I was afraid, because I was naked."* (Genesis 3:10)

Before Adam sinned God walked with Adam through the Garden of Eden. There was no fear at all, but when Adam sinned it separated sinful man from a Holy God and from that time on, man's reaction to God is fear. This fear of God is a good thing. *"The fear of the Lord is a fountain of life."* (Proverbs 14:27)

This fear is the result of man's sin and while it is proper, it was not God's original intent. God intended to be able to walk with man forever in the perfect garden He created. Man's sin ended this wonderful relationship and throughout the Bible, especially the Old Testament, we see that God's relationship with man is long distance. God comes to man in a cloud that hides all of His glory. In the New Testament we see where Jesus put away his glory and humbled himself by putting on flesh, so once again man could walk with God without fear. Once Jesus died on the cross and rose from the dead, man's sin debt was paid. Those who accept this wonderful gift of grace become children of God who no longer have to fear God, as the saints of the Old Testament did. Through the blood of Jesus we are able to talk to God as a child talks to his father.

Understand there is fear, but now our fear of God is more a sign of respect than of true fear. As a child I always loved my dad, but I also had a little fear of him, especially when I had been disobedient and was about to be punished. This is the type of fear that I believe Christians should have for our Heavenly Father, who remains our Holy God and should be viewed in reverent fear.

Adam's sin brought guilt and shame. *"And the eyes of them both were opened, and they knew that they were naked; and they sewed fig leaves together, and made themselves aprons."* (Genesis 3:7). Before Adam's sin he had no guilt or shame. He lived an amazingly peaceful and joyful life. Once he sinned he realized his nakedness and tried to cover his shame. Today we still feel the guilt and shame of sin. We spend our lives trying to cover, explain, and deny our guilt and shame.

The truth is that there is nothing we can do to separate totally from the shame and guilt of our sin. People try different things to hide their shame. They try to immerse themselves in religion by following traditions and rituals, but the guilt and shame are still there. Some devote themselves to charities that give them good feelings for a while, but soon the guilt and shame of their sin returns. Some actually embrace their guilt and shame by acting proud of it parading it around like a trophy. "Eat, drink, and be merry because tomorrow we die." "Have all the fun you can today and face the consequences later."

The reality is that a day of judgment is coming and they will face their guilt and shame. A growing number today deny their guilt and shame by denying the existence of God. If God does not exist then we are free to do anything we want free of guilt and shame. The problem with this logic is that God does exist and our sin does cause guilt and shame. All the denial in the world will not change these facts. So how do we get rid of the guilt and shame of our sin? *"Looking unto Jesus the author and finisher of our faith; who for the joy that was set before him endured the cross, despising the shame, and is set down at the right hand of the throne of God."* (Hebrews 12:2)

Jesus bore our sin, He took the guilt and shame of our sin and nailed it to the cross. This is described beautifully in Horatio Spafford's hymn, *"It is well with my soul"*. *"My sin oh the bliss of this glorious thought. My sin, not in part but the whole, is nailed to the cross, and I bare it no more, Praise the Lord, praise the Lord, O my soul."* [8] This kind of love is indescribable.

Why would God clothe himself in humanity only to be ridiculed, spat upon, mocked, and crucified? Why would the only one not deserving of guilt and shame bear all of the guilt and shame of man's sin? I do not understand this kind of love, but I certainly do accept it. Jesus took our guilt and shame, giving us the option to place all of our guilt and shame at the foot of the cross. In doing this we can live a life free of the guilt and shame of our sin. This sounds unbelievable, and it is not fair. The sad truth is that Jesus has taken all of man's guilt and shame, yet there are many who still refuse to let it go. Pride keeps many from letting go, so they spend their lives burdened by the weight of their guilt and shame. No amount of religion, good works, or pleasure will erase this, regardless of what Oprah or Dr. Phil might say. It is only by giving this guilt and shame to Jesus that you will be free of your sin. Are you holding onto your guilt and shame? If so, why not give it to Jesus? He wants to lighten your burden. After all, He has already taken it. You must simply accept it and receive it.

Adam's sin brought separation from God. *"Behold, the Lord's hand is not shortened, that it cannot save...But your iniquities have separated between you and your God, and your sins have hid his face from you that he will not hear."* (Isaiah 59:1) Before

Adam sinned God walked with Adam, but once Adam sinned it separated God from Adam. Although God searches for and makes himself known to man, the fact remains that sin has brought separation. There is nothing that we can do to restore this relationship. Although man has created religion in an attempt to restore this relationship with God, it will not work.

All of our good works and our obedience to traditions will not erase the fact that we are all sinners. This is not different from our legal system today. If I was found guilty of robbing a bank, caught on camera with a dozen eye witnesses, no amount of good works could erase my crime. I could not plea to the judge to take my good behavior into account. It would make no difference if I had been a member of the greatest church in town, or that my parents were saints, or that I had spent hours helping the needy, feeding the poor, or teaching the young...None of these things could erase my crime and I would have to serve time to pay the price for it.

This is how it works with God. He deeply desires to reestablish His relationship with sinful man, so much so that He sent His only begotten Son to pay the price for man's sin, serving to restore the relationship between Holy God and sinful man. It is because of Jesus that we have the privilege of talking to our heavenly Father in prayer, enabling us to have a relationship with God once again. This relationship will be fully restored when Jesus comes again and takes us to live with God forever in Heaven.

Adam's sin brings spiritual blindness. *"But he that hateth his brother is in darkness, and walketh in darkness, and knoweth not whither he goeth, because that darkness hath blinded his eyes."* (1 John 2:11) Sin causes man to be blind. As sinners we live in complete darkness regarding spiritual matters. One of my favorite places to visit was Mammoth Cave. It is amazing how large it is. I remember at one point during the tour, the guide turned all the lights off and we were in complete darkness. You could not see your hand in front of your face. The light was off for exactly 1 minute, but it seemed like 10 minutes. As I stood in complete darkness, I was reminded of the way sin blinds people to spiritual reality.

This is reflected by the few who honestly consider where they will spend eternity, in how lightly many treat sin, and how many see themselves as good people in no need of any relationship with God. I also remember the guide telling us that all of the creatures that live deep inside Mammoth Cave have adapted to complete darkness. People who have lived in the darkness of sin all of their lives have also adapted to their spiritual blindness. This explains how so many people do not see a need for the Bible or for church. It also explains how much sin has become not only accepted, but in many cases celebrated. Alcoholism has become such a part of society that those of us who do not drink are considered strange. Homosexuality is seen as being normal and anyone who does not accept this must be a homophobe. We use gambling to support public education, and we wonder why our kids are falling behind. We have turned killing unborn babies into a simple choice. Sin blinds us from our spiritual reality; the only source of light we have is the Word of God.

"Thy Word is a lamp unto my feet, and a light unto my path." (Psalm 119:105) The Bible sheds light into the spiritual darkness of sin and reveals God's love and grace. As I was exploring Mammoth Cave, I could not believe how beautiful it was. There were enormous crystal-like formations that would sparkle whenever light shone on them. These beautiful formations

could not be seen in the darkness. It was only when light was turned on that you could fully appreciate the true beauty of the cave.

In the same way the Bible sheds light onto God's wonderful love and grace. The more you study God's word, the more light shines. This light does a few things: it reveals God's love and grace which is wonderful, but the light of God's Word also reveals your sinful condition. This is what keeps many people from studying God's Word more intently. We love to see God's love and grace, but we do not like to see our true sinful condition. This is why so many Christians live in the shadows of God's Word. When we live in the shadows, it helps hide our sin while giving us a glimpse of God's love and grace. This is comfortable and is why I believe most Christians live in the shadow of God's Word. When you really dive into God's Word, it will reveal many things about you that are not pleasant. This is uncomfortable at first, but as the light of God's Word reveals our sin, it also reveals more and more of God's love and grace. The wonderful truth is that the bright light of God's Word reveals sin quickly, allowing you to confess that sin quickly and receive forgiveness quickly.

Let me give you a personal example. I found myself lusting after other women. I was convicted as I studied God's Word and the Holy Spirit would not let me sleep until I asked for forgiveness. I did so, and God forgave me. If I were not in God's Word I am convinced that this lusting in my heart would have continued to grow. Once this lust grew it would be more difficult to confess, and could have led to adultery and then to divorce.

The more quickly sin is identified the easier it is to confess. Understand that all sin is equal in God's eyes, but all sin does not have the same consequences. The fact that I lusted was a sin against my wife and a Holy God. The consequences involved an uncomfortable conversation with my wife which lasted a day or two. She forgave me and we moved on. Had I allowed the lust in my heart to grow, it may have led to adultery. That would have been a sin not only against a Holy God, but also my wife, my children, the other woman and her husband and children. The consequences of adultery are much worse than the consequences of lusting. Having the bright light of God's Word is so wonderful, because it will reveal sin in your heart as soon as it happens.

Sin is much like cancer in that the quicker you find it, the more likely it is to cure it. The best way to live in God's light is to stay in God's Word. Are you living in the light of God's Word, or do you like standing in the shadows of the Christian life, so you can feel comfortable with your sin while getting only a glimpse of God's love and grace?

God loves sinners and sent his Son to pay our sin debt. *"But God commendeth his love toward us, in that while we were yet sinners Christ died for the ungodly."* (Romans 5:8)

It is clear we are sinners who are born with a sinful nature and have willingly chosen to reject God to please our own selfish desires. Thankfully, this leads us to the next spiritual truth found in the Bible. God loves sinners and made a plan to send His only Son to pay the price of our sin by shedding his blood on Calvary's cross. In this section we will look at how God loves sinners, why Jesus had to shed his blood, what Jesus accomplished on the cross, what Jesus accomplished in rising from the grave, and why Jesus must return to Earth one day.

Romans 5:8 is one of my favorite verses in the Bible because it reveals a little known spiritual truth among Christians, that God really does love sinners. The spiritually-blind majority has the mistaken idea that God will reward the good and punish the sinners. The Bible teaches us that God loves sinners and that those who think they are "good enough" are in danger of spending an eternity in Hell. This is offensive to some, but wonderful news for those of us who have messed up. The truth is that when you were at your worst as a sinner, God loved you so much that He sent his only Son to die for you. God loves you in spite of your sin. God loved you when you were as far as you could get from him. This means that there is nothing you can do, good or bad to change this truth.

So many people are stuck in religion and are desperately trying to earn God's love, or keep God's love by doing good deeds and following traditions. When you truly realize that God's love for you is unconditional, it will transform how you live your life. God has already done everything that needs to be done for your salvation. You must simply place your faith in the work of His Son Jesus. He shed his blood to pay the sin debt that your endless good works can never pay.

Why did Jesus have to shed his blood to pay for our sin? *"For the life of the flesh is in the blood: and I have given it to you upon the altar to make an atonement for your souls: for it is the blood that maketh an atonement for the soul."* (Leviticus 17:11). God created life and made blood to be the source of this life. Our Holy God could have nothing to do with sin, so he had to design a way to redeem mankind. He needed something precious, and nothing is more precious than life-sustaining blood. God required a blood sacrifice as a payment for sin. This is why God accepted Abel's sacrifice of the blood of lambs but not Cain's sacrifice of plants, the fruit of Cain's labor. This foreshadows how blood, not works can bring salvation. God first established an important precedent during Passover. He required the Israelites to place the blood of an unblemished lamb on their doorposts so that the death angel sent to kill the firstborn son of Egyptian households would "Passover" their homes.

"And the blood shall be to you for a token upon the houses where ye are: and when I see the blood, I will pass over you, and the plague shall not be upon you to destroy you...ye shall keep it a feast by an ordinance forever." (Exodus 12:13-14). When the death angel came through Egypt it would look for the blood of an unblemished lamb applied to the door post. If blood was not applied, the angel would kill the firstborn son. It did not matter if those inside were religious or not, Jewish or Egyptian, rich or poor, good citizens or criminals. If the door post had the blood of an unblemished lamb on it, those inside were spared.

This powerfully illustrates how blood alone makes the difference between salvation and death. This Passover continues to be celebrated annually to remember how God freed his people from the bondage of Egyptian slavery. At the last supper Jesus celebrated a very special Passover. He identified himself as the perfect Lamb of God whose blood would redeem mankind. *"And as they were eating, Jesus took bread and blessed it, and brake it, and gave it to the disciples and said, Take eat; this is my body. And he took the cup, and gave thanks, and gave it to them saying, drink ye all of it. For this is my blood of the new testament, which is shed for many for the remission of sin."* (Matthew 26:26-28)

Jesus became the ultimate Passover lamb by sacrificing his body and shedding his blood for the remission of our sin. Today we celebrate that Passover during communion service when the faithful partake of bread, symbolizing the body of Christ and wine or juice, symbolizing the shed blood of Jesus. This is done in remembrance of Jesus' death on the cross which brought mankind salvation. It is the blood of Jesus placed in our hearts by faith that will bring salvation on Judgment day. This truth is so important. On judgment day, just as on Passover day, your religion, nationality, economic status, or good reputation will not help you. It will come down to the blood of the Lamb. Have you applied the blood of Jesus to your heart? If not, the Bible says that you will be found guilty of sin and cast into the lake of fire.

As God required the blood of an unblemished lamb during Passover, so did God require the blood of unblemished animals to be sacrificed as an atonement of sin. *"And he shall put his hand upon the head of the burnt offering; and it shall be accepted for him to make atonement for him.* (Leviticus 1:4) Before Jesus shed his blood on the cross, any sin one committed would require the blood of an innocent animal in a burnt offering ceremony. One would find an unblemished animal, usually a bullock or lamb, and would lay a hand on the animals head, transferring one's sin to the animal. The animal's neck would be cut and innocent blood would be shed to make atonement for sin.

This atonement only covered a single sin of one individual. Imagine if you had to sacrifice an animal every time you committed a sin. I am certain this would help keep the consequences of sin on your mind and in your heart. There was also an annual sin offering performed by the High Priest that would atone for Israel's sin for one year. These sacrifices were time consuming, messy and very expensive, illustrating the high cost of sin. The problem is that the blood of animals only covers man's sin and can in no way redeem man's sin. *"For it is not possible that the blood of bulls and of goats should take away sins."* (Hebrews 10:4)

Jesus became the sacrificial lamb who shed His innocent blood to pay the price of all man's sin. *"For if the blood of bulls and of goats...sanctifieth to the purifying of the flesh: How much more shall the blood of Christ."* (Hebrews 9:13-14). *"But now in Christ Jesus ye who sometimes were far off are made nigh by the blood of Christ."* (Eph.2:13) Jesus shed his perfect blood to cover all men's sin. There is only one way to Heaven according to the Bible, and that is through the precious blood of Jesus.

What did Jesus accomplish on the cross? I am certainly not qualified to fully answer this question. The cross has become the very symbol of Christianity. It is atop many church steeples, hangs on many necklaces, and adorns many of our Bibles and hymnals. Why? What did Jesus accomplish on Calvary's cruel cross? The Bible reveals at least five things Jesus accomplished on the cross. While these may not be the only things Jesus accomplished on the cross, they remain at the heart of Christianity.[9]

Jesus redeemed sinners on the cross.

"Christ hath redeemed us from the curse of the law, being made a curse for us: for it is written, cursed is everyone that hangeth on a tree." (Galatians 3:13). The most important thing Jesus did on the cross, at least from a sinner's perspective, is that he redeemed sinners from sin. Sin is in fact the curse of the law. The law was given by God and was intended to reveal the sinful

condition of man. When we read the laws of God and we are honest with ourselves, we quickly realize that we cannot follow God's law because we are sinners.

Jesus became sin on that cross. He died a sinner's death by hanging on a tree. The fact that Jesus was crucified proved for many Jews that Jesus could not be the Messiah. They did not understand what Jesus was doing by hanging on a cursed tree. He was taking on the shameful curse of sin that every one of us deserves, but will never have to endure because Jesus redeemed us.

The word redeemed was an accounting term used mostly in the slave trade. When a slave owner bought out a slave's debt it sets the slave free. Once the slave's debt had been paid he was said to be redeemed and must be set free.   The biblical word redeemed is powerful in its definition. It is God buying us back from the slavery of sin, setting us free from the bondage of sin.

I love the lyrics to the song *"redeemed"* by Big Daddy Weave. *"You look at this prisoner, and say to me son, stop fighting a fight that's already been won. And I am Redeemed! You set me free. So I'll shake off these heavy chains and wipe off every stain, now I'm not who I used to be, I am Redeemed. Thank God redeemed."* [11]

Friend, understand what Jesus did on Calvary's cruel cross was the most beautiful thing ever done in the history of man. Jesus paid the ransom we could not pay. He redeemed us despite the fact that each one of us can freely choose to reject him. In one act of selfless love, Jesus paid our ransom by shedding his blood. Through the blood of Jesus we are not only redeemed and made free from sin, we are adopted as children of God.

The Bible is Spiritually Sound.

Jesus took all of God's wrath on the cross. *"Herein is love, not that we loved God, but that He loved us, and sent His son to be the propitiation for our sins."* (1 John 4:10). Propitiation is my favorite word in the Bible, even though I cannot pronounce it to save my life. Many have wondered why God seems so much different in the Old Testament than in the New Testament. The reason in one word is propitiation.

The God of the Old Testament would often send down his wrath on sinful man. He burned Sodom and Gomorrah to the ground. He smote thousands of Philistines throughout the Old Testament, and of course he nearly destroyed Earth when He sent the flood. In the New Testament God appears so loving and full of mercy. The difference is that Jesus took all of God's wrath as he hung on the cross. This is why He cried out, *"My God, My God, Why hast thou forsaken me?"* (Matt. 27:46) When Jesus took our sin, he became sin, and Holy God was forced to turn His back on His only Son, and send all of his hatred, anger, and wrath toward sin. Think about that for a minute my friend. Imagine the power it took to destroy two cities like Sodom and Gomorrah, or the awesome power of the great flood. Jesus took all of that and more when he hung on the cross. After God had poured every bit of wrath out on his Son, Jesus said *"I thirst!"*(John 19:28), as if to say, "Is there any more wrath? Bring it!" Jesus took all the wrath of God against the sin of man and became the propitiation for our sin.

The word propitiation in Greek means to satisfy through full payment. The sin debt for all of our sins, past, present, and future were paid in full at Calvary. Understand that all sin of every man has been paid for, but not all men have accepted this wonderful gift. What a shame it is when you realize that people die and go to Hell even though their sins were already paid for by the blood of Jesus Christ.

Jesus sanctified the saints of God on the cross. *"...We are sanctified through the offering of the body of Jesus Christ once for all."* (Hebrews 10:10). Sanctification simply means to be set apart. Jesus set us apart from the sinful nature that once controlled us, and set us apart as children of God. This happened on the cross because it was on the cross that Jesus died bearing all of man's sin. So we are dead with Christ to sin and we are freed with Christ from sin. This means that sin has no more control over us as saints of God. This is important to understand because as Christians we still sin. The difference between a lost person sinning and a Christian sinning is that the Christian is sanctified. This sanctification means that sin has no power over us, because our sin has already been punished and put to death. To put another way, it is like a man who murders a room full of people and then takes his own life. That person can no longer be punished by the laws of man because he is dead. In the same way, when a Christian commits a sin he can no longer be punished for that sin because that sin has already been put to death by Jesus on the cross. Jesus bore the sins of mankind and these sins cannot be punished again. What wonderful peace comes from sanctification, as you realize the blood of Jesus has set you apart from the penalty of sin.

Jesus reconciled sinners with Our Holy Father, God on the cross. *"And having made peace through the blood of His cross, by Him to reconcile all things unto himself...And you, that were sometimes alienated and enemies in your mind by wicked works, yet now hath He reconciled in the body of His flesh through death, to present you holy and unblameable and unreproveable in His sight."* (Colossians 1:20-22). When Adam sinned in the

Garden of Eden there was a gulf created between sinful man and Holy God. There is was no way for man to bridge this gulf. God knew of only one way for man to be reconciled back to him. His son must become man, take on man's sin and pay the price of man's sin through death on a cruel cross. When Jesus took the punishment of man's sin, this paid the sin debt allowing sinful man to be made holy through the blood of Jesus Christ. Now that man is made holy, he can pursue a relationship with our Holy Creator. Jesus' death on the cross reconciled God and man for eternity.

5. **Jesus defeated Satan on the cross.** *"...That through death He might destroy him that had power of death, that is, the Devil."* (Hebrews 2:14). From the time of the Garden of Eden, God prophesied that the seed of woman, Jesus Christ, would bruise Satan's head as Satan bruised Jesus' heel. This took place on the cross. It was on the cross that Satan thought he had finally defeated Jesus. However, Jesus used the cross to pay man's sin debt, paying for man's freedom from sin, and taking away any power Satan thought he had. Satan's control over man has been taken away at the cross, Satan's control of death was taken away as Jesus rose from the dead, and Satan's control of the Earth will be taken away when Jesus returns to Earth and sits on the throne in Jerusalem. When Jesus shouted, *"It is finished"*, (John 19:30)

Satan's power was taken away as Jesus defeated sin and Satan. This does not say that sin no longer exists, but for Christians sin no longer controls us. While we still fall into sin, the penalty of sin has been paid by Jesus on the cross. This means that we are now free from the bondage of sin. As a personal example, before I was saved I was addicted to pornography. I never realized it until I was saved. Once I accepted Jesus Christ I was still drawn to pornography, but it was different. I not only knew it was wrong, I felt it was wrong. Over the years, I began turning my attention to what God's purpose for my life was, and eventually I had no desire for pornography any longer. The answer is not to try your best to quit sinning, as that does not work. The answer is to fall in love with Jesus and you will soon forget the sin that once controlled you. This happens because Jesus defeated Satan on the cross.

What did Jesus accomplish by rising from the dead? The Cross may be the symbol of Christianity, but it is the resurrection of Jesus Christ from the dead that demonstrates the power of Jesus. It is the resurrection of Christ that separates Christianity from every other religion. The resurrection of Jesus from the dead is the focus of the entire Bible. It guarantees our resurrection from the dead, and it proves beyond any doubt that Jesus is indeed the Son of God. *"The entire plan for the future has its key in the resurrection."* Billy Graham.[11]

Jesus' resurrection is the focus of the Bible. *"...I declare unto you the gospel which I preached unto you...how that Christ died for our sins...and that he was buried, and that he rose again the third day, according to the scriptures."* (1 Corinthians 15:1-4) None of us would be talking about the miraculous birth of Christ, the perfect life Christ lived, or the death of Christ on the cross were it not for the fact that Jesus rose from the dead. Paul put it best, *"If Christ be not risen, then our preaching is vain, and your faith is also vain."* (1 Corinthians 15:14)

If you remove the resurrection of Jesus from the Bible, the Bible becomes exactly what its harshest critics have suggested--an ancient book of morality that no longer is needed. However, if the resurrection of Jesus Christ happened as the Bible records, then the Bible is the only source of salvation for mankind. The resurrection of Jesus Christ validates the uniqueness of the Bible. It is not another religious book full of morality, but a powerful love story where God sends his Son to live a perfect life, only to be crucified and buried. If the story ended there it would be the world's greatest tragedy. It does not end there, however as Jesus gets up. Jesus rises from the dead and brings the world hope.

God inspired saints to write His word so that the world would know of the wonderful news that He loves us, and that one day we will live with him in glory forever. The cross reveals God's love, the resurrection gives us assurance that we will live with God forever.

Jesus' resurrection guarantees our resurrection. *"Knowing that he which raised up the Lord Jesus shall raise up us also by Jesus, and shall present us with you."* (2 Corinthians 4:14) There are many people, many religions, many helpful organizations that truly love and care for others. This is great, but just because someone loves and cares, it does not mean they have the power to truly help you eternally. Jesus may have walked around loving people, teaching wonderful truths and performing amazing miracles, but none of that really would have mattered had he not risen from the dead. When Jesus rose from the dead it proved his awesome power.

So now we not only know that Jesus loves and cares for us but he also has the power to raise us from the dead. I often put it this way, If you want to be rich one day, then I suggest you follow someone like Warren Buffet, certainly not me. If you want to be physically fit, then don't follow me, follow someone like Shaun T. If you want to be raised from the dead then there is only one person in the history of the world that has ever risen from the dead, and his name is JESUS. So many people waste their time following theories, people, or religions that may genuinely care about or love them. None has ever demonstrated the ability to raise anyone from the dead, but many place their faith in these. May I ask you what or who you are following today? Whatever it is you are following, does it have the ability to raise you from the dead? If not, why follow it? Especially when you know that Jesus not only loves you so much that he gave his life for you, He also demonstrated that he could also raise you from the dead by rising from the dead himself.

Jesus' resurrection proves His deity. *"Concerning his Son Jesus Christ our Lord, which was made of the seed of David according to the flesh. And declared to be the Son of God with Power, according to the spirit of holiness, by the resurrection from the dead."* (Romans 1:3-4) It has often been said that actions speak louder than words. I find it interesting that many critics of Jesus say that He never claimed to be God. The Bible records that Jesus said, *"I and the father are one"*. (John 10:30) and *"Before Abraham was, I AM."* (John 8:58).

He also claimed to forgive sins, which only God can do. When given a chance to deny that he claimed to be God, Jesus never denied it. *"Then said they all, Art thou then the Son of God? And HE said unto them, ye say that I am."* (Luke 22:70).

All of this has been greatly debated as to whether or not Jesus ever claimed to be God. However, what is not debated points more powerfully to Jesus being God's Son than anything Jesus may or may not have said. Jesus rose from the dead. He was brutally beaten, crucified, buried, and three days later HE GOT

The Bible is Spiritually Sound.

UP! If Jesus' resurrection from the dead does not point to Jesus claiming to be God, then nothing else could. I could claim that I am Superman, but unless I start flying, no one would believe me. Jesus not only claimed to be the Son of God with his words, He proved it by raising from the dead.

I love this quote from Timothy Keller "If Jesus rose from the dead, then you have to accept all he said; if he didn't rise from the dead, then why worry about any of what he said? The issue on which everything hangs is not whether or not you like his teaching but whether or not he rose from the dead."[12]

What will Jesus accomplish in returning again? One truth all Christians share is the fact that Jesus will return one day. That seems to be where agreement ends. Some, like me, interpret the Bible to include two separate times when Jesus is said to return. I have already discussed the rapture of the church in the prophecy chapter so I won't get too detailed here. Jesus will first return to take the church to heaven. We will sit at the Judgment Seat of Christ for our works to be judged. Those found worthy will be rewarded with crowns. We will eat at the wedding supper of the lamb, where Jesus the groom is married to His bride the church. While this takes place in Heaven, the scene is much different on Earth. God will send his wrath down onto sinful man, and through this great tribulation turn the heart of His chosen nation of Israel. As Israel is surrounded by the entire world seeking to demolish them, Israel will cry out to God. God will hear their cries and send Jesus back to Earth. Jesus' second coming will accomplish many things, all of which I am not qualified to answer, but I can speak of a few major ones here.

Jesus will return to fulfill prophecy. *"...And they shall see the Son of Man coming in the clouds of heaven with power and great glory."* (Matthew 24:30) As Jesus ascended into Heaven forty days after his resurrection, two men in white apparel predicted that Jesus will return just as He ascended. Jesus prophesied many times about returning to Earth. The Bible's prophecies always come true. Although it has been over 2000 years since Jesus last walked the Earth, the fact remains that he will one day return. Throughout history people have inaccurately tried to predict when Jesus would return. This has always intrigued me as the Bible clearly states that no one will know the time of Jesus' return. *"Watch therefore, for ye know not what hour your Lord doth come."* (Matthew 24:42).

This does not stop many from attempting to predict Jesus' return. Pope Sylvester II predicted that Jesus would return on January 1, 1000 AD. This led a mass of people to gather in Jerusalem to see Jesus set foot on the Mt. of Olives. Riots broke out when nothing happened. Christopher Columbus believed that the world began in 5343 BC and that it would only last a total of 7000 years, ending by 1658 AD. After over 100,000 people had died during the bubonic plague and due to superstitions surrounding the number 666, many believed Jesus would return in the year 1666. A group called the "Millerites" followed the teachings of William Miller who predicted Jesus would return on April 28, 1843. When He did not they revised the date to Dec. 31, 1843. Once again nothing happened, so they tried one last time and predicted Jesus would return on October 22, 1844. When Jesus never appeared they entered what they called "The Great Disappointment". Leaders of Jehovah's Witnesses set several dates when they believed Jesus would return, the first being February 13, 1925. This was revised to 1941, then again to 1975. All were obviously wrong.

 Pat Robinson predicted Jesus would come in the year 1982, and when that did not happen he revised the date to April 29, 2007. Of course, nothing has happened and yet He is still talking on television to this day.[14]

 The years of 1999 and 2000 were both widely thought to indicate the end of the world. Even the great prophet Nostradamus predicted the king of terror would come from the sky in the year 1999. Sir Isaac Newton, Jonathan Edwards, and many others wrote that Jesus would return in the year 2000.

There was even one rather legitimate concern known as the Y2K virus. People were worried that computers would crash when the date rolled over to 2000. I recall that some people stayed at work overnight in case things got crazy. Their fears were unfounded. Most recently the year 2012 was thought to be the year of Christ's return, as the Mayan calendar ran out that year. Years later, we are still here.[13]

The failed predictions of the past have led many to stop believing that Jesus will come again. Nothing could be farther from the truth. In fact the Bible does warn that in those days there will be many who doubt Jesus' return. *"Knowing this first, that there shall come in the last days scoffers, walking after their own lusts, and saying, where is the promise of his coming? For since the Fathers fell asleep, all things continue as they were from the beginning of creation."* (2 Peter 3:3-4).

This certainly seems to be the attitude of many today, but understand that God is true in his promises, Jesus will return. We must live expecting Jesus to come at any moment. This does not mean for us to look into the sky waiting for something to happen. It does mean we need to reach as many as we can with the Gospel. We should be encouraging one another and loving others. We simply do not know when Jesus is coming. I expect Jesus to come during my lifetime, but I also understand He might not come for another thousand years. Either way, this does not stop the way I try to live. Jesus is coming again, will you be ready?

Jesus will return to redeem Israel. *"And I will plant them upon their land, and they shall no more be pulled up out of their land which I have given them, saith the Lord thy God."* (Amos 9:15) Israel is unique among all the nations on Earth, as it has lived most its history outside its borders without being totally assimilated into other cultures. Israel is the only nation on Earth that inhabits the same land, bears the same name, speaks the same language, and worships the same God that it did 3,000 years ago. Joshua is credited as the first Jew to conquer the Promised Land about 1250 BC. Israel's power peaked between 1000 BC and 750 BC when Israel was ruled first by King Saul, then by David, then by Solomon. After the rule of these three kings, Israel would continue to be a nation, but not a true world power.

 Israel fell under Babylonian captivity in 587 BC. Israel ruled the Promised Land for 663 years, but would not enjoy another period of power again until May 14, 1948. For most of its history Israel has been under the rule of other world powers. The Babylonians, Persians, Greeks, Romans, the Byzantine, Arabs, Europeans, the Ottoman, and the English have all ruled over Israel.

On May 14, 1948 something miraculous happened as Israel once again ruled the Promised Land. This one event is to me the strongest evidence of fulfilled prophecy and of the certainty of the return of Jesus Christ.[14]

The book of Revelation tells us that in the last days the anti-Christ will lead the world's armies against Israel and attempt to destroy God's chosen nation. It is then that Israel cries out to God for help and God hears the cries of his chosen people and sends His Son Jesus Christ to redeem Israel. *"And I saw heaven opened, and behold a white horse; and he that sat upon him was called Faithful and True…And the armies which were in heaven followed him,…and out of his mouth goeth a sharp sword, that with it he should smite the nations: and he shall rule them with a rod of iron…and on his thigh a name written, King of Kings, and Lord of Lords."* (Revelations 19:11-16)

It is at this moment that Israel finally sees Jesus as the Messiah and they turn back to God a redeemed people. Jesus will then rule the world from His throne in Jerusalem for a thousand years of peace like the world has never known. *" …they lived and reigned with Christ 1000 years. But the rest of the dead lived not again until the 1000 years were finished…but they shall be priests of God and of Christ, and shall reign with Him a 1000 years."* (Revelations 20:4-6). Jesus will one day rule the world from the redeemed nation of Israel for a thousand years of peace.

Jesus will return to redeem God's creation. *"For the earnest expectation of the creature waiteth for the manifestation of the Sons of God…Because the creature itself also shall be delivered from the bondage of corruption into the glorious liberty of the children of God. For we know that the whole creation groaneth* *and travaileth in pain together until now."* (Romans 8:19-22) When Adam first sinned in the Garden of Eden, the curse of sin was placed on the Earth. From that time onward this Earth has been full of pain and suffering. Many people question why God allows suffering, and most do not like the answer: it is our sin. God created a perfect world, with no suffering, no pain, and no death. Man's choice to satisfy himself rather than obey God cursed the world which brought suffering, pain, and death. God knew that this would happen and sent His Son to become man, suffer and shed his precious blood, paying the price of man's sin and redeeming all creation.

One of my favorite books is "The reason for God" by Timothy Keller. In the book he deals with some of life's most difficult questions one of which is why does God allow suffering? I love this quote from Keller " If it is true, how can God be a God of love if he does not become personally involved in suffering the same violence, oppression, grief, weakness, and pain that we experience? The answer to that question is twofold. First, God can't. Second, only one major world religion even claims that God does."[8]

While Jesus' crucifixion and resurrection redeemed God's creation, it will not come to fruition until Jesus returns. When Jesus returns, God's entire creation will be drastically transformed. The lion will sleep with the lamb, and there will be no more storms, earthquakes, tornadoes, or hurricanes (not even zombie apocalypses).

It will be as if man had never sinned. I cannot wait to see this perfect world as Jesus returns to redeem God's creation.

Jesus will return to reward the faithful. *"And behold, I come quickly; and my reward is with me, to give every man according* *as his work shall be."* (Revelation 22:12). These are the last words of Jesus recorded in the Bible. They reveal the heart of Jesus, which desires to reward those who have faithfully followed Him. As a good Southern Baptist I am well aware that grace, not works save but the Bible is clear that works matter. We are saved to do good works, we do not do good works to become saved.

However there appears to be a troubling trend in the church that people live however they wish without regard to how they live. After all, we are saved by grace. This is a dangerous way to live. We should have a deep desire to obey Jesus Christ because He has loved us so much. Our works should flow from our love for Christ and for others. Anything that we do motivated by love will be rewarded, anything we do for ourselves will not last. The Bible is clear that we will be given rewards in heaven. The rewards we are given will determine our role during the millennial reign of Christ.

The Bible gives us a hint as to how people will be rewarded, *"But many that are first shall be last; and the last shall be first."* (Matthew 19:30). *"Blessed are the meek for they shall inherit the Earth."* (Matthew 5:5). These verses were spoken by Jesus and they suggest that those who humbly serve others will one day become rulers on the Earth. This has obviously never happened, but when Jesus returns and establishes his millennial kingdom it certainly will. Jesus is waiting to reward those who are faithful to him. What rewards await you in heaven?

Sinners must place faith in Jesus Christ. *"That if thou shalt confess with thy mouth the Lord Jesus, and shalt believe in thine heart that God hath raised him from the dead, thou shalt be saved.. "* (Romans 10:9) Most all Christians agree that faith in

Jesus Christ is needed for salvation. There is often disagreement on what exactly saving faith is.

The faith that saves. *"For by grace are ye saved through faith; and not of yourselves: it is the gift of God. Not of works, lest any man should boast."* (Ephesians 2:8-9)

What must we do to be saved? This important question has different answers depending on who you talk to. I remember being taught the six steps to salvation: 1. Hear the word, 2. Believe the Word, 3. Repent of your sins, 4. Confess Jesus Christ as your Savior, 5. Obey Jesus in Baptism, and 6. Live a Christian life. These are all found in the Bible and I still accept these steps as important parts of the Christian faith. The problem is these steps are a way to satisfy my selfish pride by giving me a list to check off so that I might earn my salvation.

The question, *"What must I do to be saved?"* is not the best question to ask, as it implies that there is something one must accomplish to earn salvation. The better question is: *"What has God done to provide salvation to me as a hopeless sinner?"* Ephesians 2:8-9 includes four aspects of salvation that are important to understand: grace, faith, the gift of God, and that it is not about works. We will look closely at each aspect to see how to answer the important question of what we must we do to be saved?

Salvation is the gift of God. *"For the wages of sin is death; but the gift of God is eternal life through Jesus Christ our Lord."* (Romans 6:23) Salvation was planned by God from the beginning. God has predestined everyone to be saved. God has not predestined anyone to burn in Hell. We are sinners by nature and each of us has chosen to rebel against our Holy Creator, therefore we all deserve death. Thankfully, God has given the world a wonderful gift, eternal life in Heaven. God's gift is not cheap, as it was paid for by the blood of Jesus Christ. Salvation cannot come any other way. This gift of God did not come about by chance. The Bible tells us that from the beginning, even before creation, God planned to redeem mankind. *"According as he hath chosen us in him before the foundation of the world, that we should be holy and without blame before him in love."* (Ephesians 1:4)

This verse has several implications, the first being that salvation comes from God. God chose us by creating each of us to have an eternal relationship with him. His desire is for to become holy. If we are not holy, it is impossible for us to have a relationship with our Holy creator. The problem is that we are hopeless sinners who on our own will never become holy. That is why God provided a way for each one of us to be saved before he even created us. This is what is meant by predestination. People have distorted the definition of predestination to mean that God selects some to go to heaven and others to burn in hell.

This certainly is not consistent with what much of the Bible teaches. *"For this is good and acceptable in the sight of God our Savior; who will have all men to be saved, and to come unto the knowledge of the truth."* (1 Timothy 2:3-4).

"The Lord is not slack concerning His promise...but is longsuffering to us-ward, not willing that any should perish, but that all should come to repentance." (2Peter 3:9).

"For God so loved the world that He gave his only begotten Son, that whosoever believeth in him should not perish, but have everlasting life." (John 3:16).

The Bible is Spiritually Sound.

It is clear to me that God loves everyone and not only desires that all men be saved, He has done everything possible to provide a way for every person to be saved. The idea that God would predestine people to burn in Hell is simply unbiblical. I realize that you can take verses out of context which seem to indicate this, but I find it imperative to step back and see the Bible's overriding message, love for all men. Does this mean that everyone will go to Heaven? No, while God has provided a way for all to be saved, and He desires that all will be, the truth is not all will accept God's wonderful gift of salvation. There are many who simply refuse to surrender their will to God, and they will stubbornly go to Hell. The only way anyone will go to Hell is by willingly stepping through the blood of Jesus. God will never force His will on anyone, but He has provided a way for all to be saved.

The fact that God chose us from the foundation of the world also implies that God loved you before you ever thought about loving Him. It means that while you were living in sin, God loved you. It means that no matter how you view yourself, or how others view you, God sees all of your faults and loves you anyway. This is a powerful truth. How I wish you could see the depths of God's love for you, my friend. God sees what he created you to be, and He has not given up on you. Why waste your life trying to satisfy your selfish desires, and instead accept God's wonderful will for your life. He has already chosen you, and He wants to give you the wonderful gift of salvation. Have you accepted God's gift? If not, will you accept it today?

Works will not work when it comes to salvation. *"But we are all as an unclean thing, and all our righteousnesses are as filthy rags; and we all do fade as a leaf, and our iniquities, like the wind, have taken us away."*(Isaiah 64:6) We are prideful by nature and Satan appeals to that pride. He attempts to convince us that we can be godlike if we try hard enough. In fact, this idea is what separates Christianity from all other religions. Other religions teach that if you follow certain laws and keep certain traditions, if you simply do what you are told, you will earn God's love. The problem with this is that we are sinners who simply cannot live perfect lives. The idea that God will take our good works and weigh them against our bad works may be popular, but it will not happen that way. This type of judgment never takes place in our own judicial system.

If I were to be caught on camera robbing a bank, and I were standing before the judge and tried to convince him that my good works outweighed my one poor decision to rob the bank, how would that influence his ruling? If he were a just judge it would not affect his judgment at all. The same is true with God. If we are guilty of one sin, we are sinners and deserve the punishment of sin which is death. *"For whosoever shall keep the whole law, and yet offend in one point, he is guilty of all."* (James 2:10). Do you understand that you only need to be guilty of one sin to be a sinner, in the same way you only have to kill one person to be a murderer? No amount of good works will change that.

For the sake of argument, let's assume for a moment we could earn our salvation by doing good works, or keeping moral laws or following religious traditions. If that were so, why would God allow Jesus to be crucified? When Jesus was suffering on the cross and praying that God remove the weight of sin from him, do you not believe that God would have relented if He believed there was another way we could earn salvation? The fact is that we have absolutely no chance of being good enough for salvation; instead it is the gift of a loving God. Our pride makes this fact hard to accept. That is why most people, even Christians, try to mix works with grace and faith when it comes to salvation. We would like a nice little checklist to mark off whether we did it or not.

The Bible does not include any checklist for salvation. Our pride approves of lists like these, so we can check them and believe as if we have somehow accomplished our own salvation. The truth is salvation comes from God and must simply be accepted by us, not accomplished by us.

Grace not works save. *"And if by grace, then is it no more of works: otherwise grace is no more grace."* (Romans 11:6)

I like John T. Yates' definition of Grace as the undeserved love and unmerited favor of God apart from any works of righteousness or merit. Grace is based entirely upon the sacrificial death of Jesus Christ. Works depends on your righteousness, while grace rejects your righteousness and gives you the righteousness of God. Our pride has a hard time understanding the grace that the Bible teaches. Many view this type of grace as cheap grace, believing that teaching this type of grace leads to living life with a license to sin. The Apostle Paul understood this reasoning and dealt with it, *"What shall we say then? Shall we continue in sin that grace may abound? God forbid."* (Romans 6:1-2)

Grace does not free us to sin, it frees us from sin. Grace does not foster sin, it forgives sin. To be honest, I struggled with grace until I heard John T. Yates begin to describe how living under grace compares with to living by works. Grace understands that salvation is a gift of love from God, while works understand salvation as our ability to keep God's law.

The Bible is Spiritually Sound.

Let's take a moment to compare a life motivated by love, versus a life trying to keep the law. [15]

When you are motivated by law, you try to determine the least you can do and yet be within the law. Take taxes as an example. We are all motivated by law to pay our taxes. However, we pay tax experts to help us find the least amount we must pay to stay within the law. This is how the law always works. Take a speeding limit as another example. If the speed limit is 65, we will drive as fast as we can without getting a ticket. I will often go 5 to 10 miles over the speed limit, hoping not to get pulled over.

 When Christians are motivated by keeping the law they often asked questions like: *"How many times do I need to pray? How much money do I have to tithe? How often should I go to church? What must I do to be saved and remain saved?* These questions all suggest that every aspect of Christianity is a chore. What is the least I can do and still get into Heaven? No wonder so many Christians mope around under the burden living a certain way to get into Heaven. When you are motivated by the law and works, you can quickly become discouraged, exhausted, and burned out. This is the reason so many Christians tend to fall in and out of church.

 Let me ask you a question, "What is it you love doing?" I'll tell you what I love--college football! (Roll Tide!) Because I love college football I will get up early on my day off, drive over three hours one way and sit in the hot sun, the pouring rain, or chilly night to watch football for nearly four hours. Then I sit in horrible traffic and drive nearly five hours back home, never complaining. In fact I enjoy every minute of it and look forward to doing it again. If it were something I did not love and someone told me I had to get up early on my day off, drive over three hours one way, sit in the hot sun for four hours, deal with horrible traffic, and drive nearly five hours home, I would be miserable.

When you are motivated by love it changes everything. If you have children, let me ask you, do you look for the cheapest gifts to give your children? Do you dread spending time with them? I bet you don't. I bet you search for the best gifts for your children and you cherish time spent with them. I talk to other parents who are excited about spending long weekends watching their children play baseball, gymnastics, band, tennis, soccer, or dance. If those same parents were required by law to spend long weekends away from home I bet none would be excited.

 This is the difference between being motivated by love and grace to please God, rather than being motivated by the law and required works. When Christians are motivated by the law and find themselves working to please God, they often complain and burn out. When Christians are motivated by love as a result of the wonderful gift of grace, they get excited about church, missions, and even tithing. What motivates you as a Christian? Do you view going to church as something you must do to please God or do you view church as an opportunity to worship the one you love and enjoy the sweet fellowship of other believers? I challenge you to quit trying to please God with actions, and simply fall in love with the God who shares his loving gift of grace with you.

How does faith save? *"So then faith come by hearing, and hearing by the word of God."* (Romans 10:17) Faith has been considered a central theme in salvation among all religions. The majority of people would say it is faith that is needed to get to heaven. The problem is that most feel that faith is all you need for salvation. The more faith you have the better chance you will be saved. So it is important to keep the faith, because everyone needs something to believe in. When a person loses faith, he will lose hope and become depressed, disillusioned, and ultimately defeated. Everyone advises you to keep the faith, that everyone needs something to believe in and that's what ultimately matters. Experts today will advise you to just find something, or someone, to place your faith in and everything will be fine. This philosophy is absurd. I contend it is not the amount of faith you have, it is the object of your faith that makes all the difference. Let me give you a couple of examples of the difference between a lots of faith in the wrong thing versus a little faith in the right thing.

Not too long ago I visited the Titanic museum in Pigeon Forge, Tennessee and it was a great experience. When you first enter the museum you are given a card with the name of a real passenger of the Titanic, as well as what class they were in and a little about them. At the end of the tour, you find out whether or not they survived. The person I got was a mail carrier who did not survive. The Titanic was considered the finest passenger ship to ever sail the seas, virtually unsinkable. The 2201 people fortunate enough to cruise on the Titanic no doubt had tremendous faith that they would make it safely to New York. However, all their faith did not matter as the Titanic sank about two and a half hours after hitting an iceberg.

Compare this with those who were aboard the Ark. Noah had never sailed one day in his life yet he and three sons built an Ark that would have to remain afloat during the world's worst flood. Now the Bible does not say this, but I can only imagine the fear of Noah's wife in particular, as she had to place her faith in an Ark built by her husband and three sons.

I can only imagine how my wife Emily would react if she had to climb in a boat built by me and my three boys! We have never built so much as a dog house. My bet would be that she would take her chances with a pool noodle. Despite Noah's wife probable lack of faith she survived. You see how it's the object of your faith and not so much the amount of your faith that will save you.

Here is another example: a couple of years ago #1 Alabama was ahead of #5 Auburn 21-7 at halftime and I had all the faith in the world that Alabama would win that game. However, Auburn came back in the second half to tie the game 28-28. With 1 second left in the game, Alabama attempted a 57 yard field goal (don't ask me why) and of course he misses. I thought the game would go to overtime and Alabama would win, but the craziest thing happened as an Auburn player caught the ball deep in the end-zone and returned it 109 yards for the game winning touchdown, to the amazement of the Auburn fans, who no doubt had only a shred of faith that Auburn would actually win. On the other hand, I sat in shock as Alabama actually lost the game despite my great faith that they would win.

Again it is not the amount of faith that matters, but the object of the faith that makes all the difference. *"If ye had faith as great as a mustard seed, ye might say unto this Sycamore tree, be thou plucked up by the root, and be thou planted by the sea; and it should obey you."* (Luke 17:6).

While it is certainly important to have faith, it is the object of your faith that determines whether or not your faith is the kind that saves. There is no doubt that the majority of Muslims

208

demonstrate much more faith than the average Christian in America. Muslims pray five times a day, dress modestly, attend services at their mosques, and most of them make a pilgrimage to Mecca every year. The average Christian may attend church for 1 hour Sunday morning, and pray before they go to bed, if they aren't too tired. If it were the amount of faith that mattered, the Muslims would be way ahead of most Christians, but since it is the object of our faith that matters, nearly 2 billion Muslims are in danger of losing their souls because they have placed their faith in the wrong things.

Muslims are not the only ones who have misplaced their faith. There are a countless numbers of *"Christian"* people who sit in church and place their faith in a religion, a church, a pastor, or a priest and are no more saved than those who have never attended church. Others scoff at religion and place their faith in the knowledge of man, in modern science and philosophy or physics; this faith will not save either. Still others place their faith in family, career, sports, entertainment, politics, drugs, or any number of other things that will not bring salvation. There is only one object of faith that can save and his name is Jesus Christ. Jesus said, *"I am the way, the truth, and the life, no one comes to the Father but by me."* (John 14:6).

Those who place their faith in anything else will perish. It only takes the amount of faith of a mustard seed to be saved if that faith is placed in the correct place, which the Bible teaches is Jesus Christ. Salvation is a gift of God and is something that must be accepted and not accomplished. You can do nothing to earn salvation; you must however place your faith in the one who provides salvation--Jesus Christ. Where have you placed your faith?

Once saved, we should live a life of love. [1]*"Even so faith, if it hath not works, is dead, being alone."* (James 2:17)

Living the Christian Life. *"I beseech you therefore brethren, by the mercies of God, that ye present your bodies a living sacrifice, holy, acceptable unto God, which is your reasonable service. And be not conformed to this world: but be ye transformed by the renewing of your mind that ye may prove what is that good and acceptable, and perfect will of God."* (Romans 12:1-2) God has created us, forgiven us, redeemed us, and made us his beloved children we owe it to God to worship Him. This is a natural response. However, many Christians view worship as singing praise songs to God. While God certainly loves to hear our praises in song, this is not what the Bible describes as worship. True worship, according to the Bible is making ourselves available to God, surrendering our will to God's will.

In Jefferson Bethke's book Jesus > Religion he tells an old story about Abraham Lincoln buying back a slave from the marketplace. He saw her in bondage and was compelled to set her free. When the chains were removed she goes up to Lincoln and asks what he wants from her. He simply replies "your free". She exclaims "I'm free to do anything I want?" "Yes, whatever you want." She then says with a smile "If I truly am free to do anything I want, then I'm following you." Bethke comments " When you understand how great the gift you have been given by Jesus is, you can't help but follow him" [16]

 We are to offer ourselves as living sacrifices to God. When I think about living sacrifices I am reminded of the time God asked Abraham to sacrifice his son Isaac. This story may seem cruel and unthinkable but it is really a beautiful picture of Jesus being sacrificed by God for each of us.

We often picture Isaac as a little boy, but it is more likely that Isaac was much older. Some Biblical scholars say he may have been as old as thirty, but most place Isaac's age as in his teens, as he was able to carry the wood for the sacrifice up a mountain. Abraham was a very old man at this time, well over 100 years old. Picture this: a 100 year old man takes a teenager and binds him to the altar. Would Abraham have been able to tie down a grown man to the alter and keep him there long enough to burn him alive? That could happen only if Isaac allowed himself to be tied down to the altar. This is what happened that day, as Abraham took his son Isaac to be a sacrifice to God. Isaac carried the wood for the sacrifice, laid down on the altar and allowed his father Abraham to bind him to the altar. If Isaac had not wanted to be tied down to an altar and sacrificed, his 100 year old father could not have possibly whipped his 20 year old son and tied him to an altar. Isaac willingly laid down on the altar and allowed Abraham to tie him to the altar.

This is a clear picture of Jesus who also carried his cross and allowed sinful man to nail him to a cross. *"Therefore doth my Father love me, because I lay down my life, that I might take it again. No man taketh it from me, but I lay it down of myself..."* John 10:17-18) The difference is God spared Isaac, but did not spare His own Son. This is the kind of living sacrifice that shows the type of worship God desires. We must make ourselves available to God. We do this in a couple of ways: 1. We obey God's commands. 2. We keep away from the sinful world. 3. This strengthens our faith.

The clearest way to worship God is to obey His commands. What are God's commands for Christians? *"Go ye therefore, and teach all nations, baptizing them in the name of the Father, and of the Son, and of the Holy Ghost.* (Matthew 28:19). Here we have Jesus' final commands for his disciples. We are commanded to go and teach others the gospel of Christ. This word *"go"* is best interpreted as *"as you go"*, which indicates that we be ready to share the gospel wherever we go. Most Christians rarely, if ever, share the Gospel with anyone. This is clearly willful disobedience to the command of Jesus Christ. Spreading the Gospel was never intended to be limited to those called to preach or to be missionaries, all Christians are to go. This does not require you to leave your town, or even your house these days. You can share the gospel so easily today by calling, texting, or Facebooking.

My fourteen year old son Jonathan is addicted to video games, as are most boys his age, but I was proud of him as I overheard him sharing the Gospel to someone in Germany who was playing with him on line. He never got off the sofa, yet he was being obedient. For most Christians we simply need to be prepared to share the Gospel wherever we go: the grocery store, gas station, restaurant, sporting event, work, or even playing video games. We may be lead to something more, like short term missions, or working in a homeless shelter, nursing home, or prison, or we may be called to pastor a church, or go into the mission field. Whatever it is we must obey Jesus' clear command to go. When is the last time you shared the Gospel? Why don't you make certain you are prepared to share the Gospel as you go about your life this week?

"Beloved, if God so loved us, we ought also to love one another". (1 John 4:11) God demonstrated his love toward us by sending his Son to die on the cross for our sins. As we have received such love, we should in turn love others. We were saved not simply to keep us from Hell, but to be God's presence in this sin-

filled world. How will the world recognize us as being Christian if we do not first demonstrate true love? The answer is that they will not. One of the reasons so many people have a hard time believing in God is that we as Christians have failed to demonstrate love. When we as Christians gossip, gripe or curse others, it not only fails to demonstrate God's love, it hurts those who may be looking to us as Christians for encouragement.

Earlier I talked about the importance of spreading the Gospel wherever we are living our lives. However, if we are not demonstrating the love of God by our actions and words, very few will listen, even if the words may be true. When we as Christians proclaim Jesus with our lips but deny him by our lifestyle, we make it very difficult for a lost and dying world to accept what we say.

If this world is ever going to be brought back to God, we as Christians need to get up out of our pews and get busy loving others. The problem is that most Christians have either accepted the world's insistence that we tolerate others, or they stubbornly sit in their pews in church and condemn others the way Christians did hundreds of years ago. Very few Christians take the time and effort to love others. There is a major difference between tolerating others, condemning others and loving others. All you have to do to tolerate someone is absolutely nothing. Tolerate means that we sit back and let people do whatever they want, without concern.

Imagine what would happen if you were to simply tolerate your children. If your kids are like mine they would eat nothing but pop tarts, they would sit all day and play video games, and they might not ever brush their teeth or take a bath. They would not go to school or church. They would just do whatever they desired and never learn responsibility, accountability, or feel genuinely loved. This is what has happened to society. The church has tolerated others and allowed society to drift farther and farther from God. The world has confused tolerance with love, believing that if you love someone you allow them to do whatever feels good, even when you know the Bible teaches that many things that feel good are not good at all.

What if you lived near a bridge that had been washed out and you knew that any car driving too fast would fall over into a flooded river? Would love be demonstrated by sit on your front porch and waving as cars went flying by? Of course it wouldn't, yet this is what we are doing as Christians by tolerating the sinful behavior of the world. We are waving politely as people speed by to their eternal deaths. The problem is that many Christians are afraid that people may not like us if we try to warn them about the consequences of their sin.

Again, how do we show our children love? Do we worry that they may not like us if we make them stop playing games and do their homework? Not if we love them. When you love someone you will often have to do or say things that may be difficult, but if we truly love our friends we will tell them. Sure this may result in some awkward moments, but is that not better than allowing your friends to destroy their lives? Love is the key.

There are Christians who have no problem pointing out their friends' problems. In fact they enjoy condemning others. We rarely condemn others because we love them, we condemn others because it makes us feel superior. This kind of attitude is just as bad as tolerance. What if all you did is condemn your children? They would feel inadequate, insecure, and unloved.

The Bible is Spiritually Sound.

This is how many feel today. As Christians we must acknowledge sin as sin, but we must do this in love and not in a condescending, condemning way.

Loving others is difficult. The secret to the kind of love the Bible teaches is to understand how God demonstrated His love toward us. God did not tolerate our sinful behavior, allowing us to do whatever we want with no consequences. Nor did God condemn our sinful behavior and send us directly to Hell as punishment for our rebellious behavior. God demonstrated his love toward us by sending His only begotten Son to die on a cross to pay the sin debt that we could never pay. Love is difficult and takes sacrifice. As Christians we know how to love others because we understand that God first loved us.

Faith that works. *"Even so faith, if it hath no works is dead, being alone."* (James 2:17) Many Bible scholars believe that there are conflicting ideas between James and Paul. James seems to say that you must have works to truly have faith, while Paul often teaches that works can in no way bring salvation. We have discussed how Ephesians 2:8-9 teaches that salvation is a gift of God that must be accepted by faith, apart from works. If you read the very next verse I think it will clear up some of this confusion. *"For we are His workmanship, created in Christ Jesus unto good works..."* (Ephesians 2:10).

It seems clear that James and Paul agree that if you have the type of faith that saves, it will be accompanied by works or it is not saving faith. Once a person places his faith in Jesus, he is given the gift of the Holy Spirit which motivates us to do good works. These good works help produce what Jesus describes as fruit. If you as a Christian bear no fruit then you may not truly be a Christian. You must understand that works can in no way bring salvation, but once you place your faith in the blood of Jesus Christ you should demonstrate good works.

As Christians we are not expected to produce good works in order to keep our salvation. This is what many teach, but it is not Biblical. *"And I give unto them eternal life and they shall never perish, neither shall any man pluck them out of my hand."* (John 10:28) I grew up believing that I could lose my salvation, so I tried my best to produce enough good works to stay saved. This is no different from trying to do enough good works to get saved. If I could not earn my salvation by following God's law, how could I stay saved if that salvation depends on my ability to follow Jesus?

The Bible clearly states that we are eternally saved. Jesus states that He holds our salvation in his hand and no man can pluck that away. I remember being taught that no outside force could take your salvation away, but you could choose to lose it by living in sin. As I look back at that reasoning, I find it hard to believe I ever thought that. If Jesus clearly states that no man can take salvation out of his hand, then how could I believe that somehow I could break Jesus' grip on my soul?

Another misconception is that if Jesus gave us eternal life that we could lose, it would not really be eternal life would it? Notice what Paul says, *"Being confident of this very thing, that He which hath begun a good work in you will perform it until the day of Jesus Christ."* (Philippians 1:6)

It was God who planned your salvation, it was Jesus who provided your salvation, and it is the Holy Spirit that protects your salvation. God as the Trinity has done it, is doing it, and will make certain it is done. When we doubt our salvation, we may think we humbly accept the fact that we still struggle with sin, when actually we doubt the ability of the blood of Jesus to forgive our sin.

If works do not bring salvation nor do they help us keep salvation then why do good works? There is a great little book by Bruce Wilkinson entitled *"Secrets of the Vine"* that dives into Jesus parable' of the vine and the branches and describes how good works are expected from every Christian. Listen to Jesus' words: *"I am the vine, ye are the branches: He that abideth in me, and I in him, the same bringeth forth much fruit: for without me ye can do nothing."* (John 15:5). [17]

When you get the picture of what Jesus is describing, hopefully it will transform how you live your life. Jesus is the vine which brings life to all the branches. God is the vinedresser who cares for the entire grapevine. His desire is for every branch to produce fruit. He walks through the vineyard looking for branches not producing fruit. Some branches have fallen in the dirt, so the vinedresser reaches down, picks them up and gently ties them onto a trellis to keep the branches from the dirt so they can produce fruit. He prunes any branches that are not producing so they will be fruitful. Christians are the branches. Some are long and full of leaves, weighing branches down and forcing the branch into the dirt where it is unable to produce fruit. The fruit represents good works, things a Christian does motivated by love of God and others.[17]

This illustration is amazingly descriptive of how Christian life works. Jesus gives every branch life which allows the branch to produce fruit. This demonstrates how it is actually Jesus who gives us the ability to do good works. This allows us to remain humble as we understand that we have actually done nothing apart from Christ. I find it interesting that branches that are the longest and are full of leaves do not produce much fruit and often end up stuck in the mud unable to produce.

This illustrates Christians whose lives are so consumed with the things of the world that they spend them trying to satisfy their selfish desires and neglecting God's purpose for their lives. These Christians often live in sin, making it very difficult for these Christians to do good works. What is wonderful is that God is pictured as the vinedresser who searches the vineyard for any fallen branches. When He finds a fallen branch, He gently takes it, cleans it, prunes it and ties it to a trellis enabling the branch to once again produce fruit.

The secret of the vine is to allow God to prune you often and resist the temptation to allow your leaves to grow and take away from your ability to produce fruit. What does this kind of life surrendered to God look like? *"For it is God which worketh in you both to will and to do his good pleasure. Do all things without murmurings and disputings: That ye may be blameless and harmless, the Sons of God, without rebuke, in the midst of a crooked and perverse nation, among whom you shine like stars."* (Philippians 2:13-15) When you are totally surrendered to God in Faith and you allow God to prune your life, you will begin to produce much fruit. This allows your life to shine, pointing people to God.

Many Christians refuse to allow God to prune them. They want just enough Jesus to save them but none of the Jesus that changes them. These Christians miss the whole point of salvation, which is to be molded by Jesus. The funny thing is that Jesus will change you, but not like many think. I love the story that my pastor Joel Sutherland shared last Sunday. Joel was golfing when he noticed a carpenter who was working on his house, so Joel invited this carpenter to join him. The only thing he knew about the man was that he was a highly recommended carpenter, but as they began to play he noticed he was an excellent golfer. Joel would hit balls into the woods, into the lake, everywhere but the hole, while this carpenter was making birdies. As they continued golfing Joel began to ask for advice about golf and by the 18th hole, Joel's golf game had been totally transformed.

You see most Christians only know Jesus as the Son of God who died on the cross for their sins. This is very important to know but it is only basic knowledge. In order to know Jesus you must spend time with him and as you do, you begin to see how wonderful he is and how He can change your life if you let Him. The closer you get to Jesus, the more He will transform your life into the joy-filled peaceful life you have desired since you accepted Christ as Savior.

The problem is we often do not want to be changed. We simply want to know Jesus as our fire insurance to keep us out of Hell, but we are not interested in knowing Him enough for Him change us. When we get to the point as Christians where we ask Jesus to change us and make us more mature and effective Christians, we will begin to see how much Christ can use us. This is exactly what living the Christian life is all about, growing closer and closer to Jesus Christ. Jesus said, *"I have come that they might have life, and that they might have it more abundantly."* (John 10:10)

Jesus wants to change our lives, prune us not to punish us, but so that we can enjoy the more abundant life God created us for. Just as the golfer changed Joel's golf swing which greatly improved his game, Jesus wants to change us so that we can live a blessed life that produces much fruit for God's kingdom. Are you living a life of faith, motivated by a deep love for God and others? If you feel that you are missing the abundant life Jesus speaks about, you must allow yourself to be changed. You must deepen your relationship with God.

When we realize who God is and what God has done for us, it should motivate us to obey Him. We should be like Isaiah who simply told God *"Here am I send me."* (Isaiah 6:8) This is the only response we as sinners should have before an almighty God. When we are asked to do something for someone else, our response will not depend on the difficulty of the request but on how much we value the one making the request.

There are times just as I lay my head on my pillow that my wife will remember she left her phone in the car, and she will ask me to get up, go out to the car and get her phone. This is not something I would even consider if anyone else asked me to get up from my bed just after I finally laid my head down. It is because of my deep love for my wife that I will get out of bed, search for my keys, put on my shoes, and go out to the car to retrieve my sweet wife's phone.

Once again, I lay my head on the pillow to finally get some rest, and just as I begin to doze off I hear a voice down the hall, *"I'm thirsty!"* I roll over and hope my sweet wife will get up and check on our daughter. *"I'm thirsty!" As* Emily nudges me I get up out of my nice warm bed again, go down the stairs to the kitchen, pour a glass of water, go back up the stairs to my daughter Kathryn's room to give her the water and kiss her goodnight. Why would I do this? It is not because I enjoy getting out of bed that I do these things, it is because of my love for my wife and my children. In the same way we as Christians ought to stand ready to obey our loving Father God.

Love is the key to the Christian life. We are often caught up in the thou shalt's and the thou shall not's of the Bible rather than focusing on simply loving others. I love what Peter says here . *"And above all things have fervent charity among yourselves: for charity shall cover the multitude of sins."* (1 Peter 4:8) Think about that for a moment...Love covers a multitude of sins. It is impossible to live your life trying to keep all the commandments found in the Bible, it is much easier to simply love God and love people. The great thing is that when we love God and love people we end up keeping the Bible's commandments anyway.

The Bible is the truth of an almighty God. Every word of it is true. It is true in every way.You may disagree with some of the points I have made. My goal was never to get you to agree with my thoughts and opinions, my goal is to lift up the Word of God. I hope you spend more time in God's Word and I encourage you to see for yourself how wonderful the Bible is. May God bless you as you simply take God at His Word.

Life can often become overwhelming and we need to be encouraged from time to time. When I find myself in need of some encouragement I turn to the Psalms. Here are a few of my favorite Psalms that have helped me and may hopefully help you as well.

Psalm 3: When people have come against you...*"The Lord is my shield and lifter of my head."*

Psalm 8: When you doubt God...*"When I consider thy heavens..."*

Psalm 16: When you doubt your future...*"Thou wilt show me the path of life..."*

Psalm 23: Anytime...*"The Lord is my Shepherd..."*

Psalm 34: When you are depressed...*"I will bless the Lord at all times..."*

Psalm 40: When you are hopeless...*"I am poor and needy, yet the Lord thinketh upon me."*

Psalm 46: When you are afraid...*"God is our refuge and strength..."*

Psalm 51: When you are in need of forgiveness...*"Have mercy upon me, Oh God..."*

Psalm 63: When you need to talk with God...*"My soul thirsteth for thee..."*

The Bible is Spiritually Sound.

Psalm 66: Understand God's faithfulness..."*make a joyful noise unto God.*"

Psalm 73: When the wicked prosper..."*I was envious of the foolish...*"

Psalm 94: When you need to feel secure..."*God is the rock of my refuge*"

Psalm 100: When you are thankful..."*Make a joyful noise unto the Lord...*"

Psalm 103: Give God praise..."*Bless the Lord Oh my Soul...*"

Psalm 111: Give God more praise..."*Praise ye the Lord.*"

Psalm 116: God hears your prayers..."*I love the Lord, because he hath heard my voice...*"

Psalm 121: God will give you help..."*My help cometh from the Lord.*"

Psalm 128: God blesses the faithfull..."*Blessed is everyone that feareth the Lord.*"

Psalm 139: God knows your situation. "*O Lord, thou hast searched me, and known me*"

Psalm 142: When you need a shoulder to cry on..."*I cried unto the Lord...*"

The Bible is Spiritually Sound.

Here are a few of my favorite New Testament Chapters:

Romans 8 : *"There is therefore now on condemnation to them which are in Christ Jesus."*

1 Corinthians 15: *"For as in Adam all die, even so in Christ shall all be made alive."*

Ephesians 2: *"For by grace are ye saved through faith, and that not of yourself, it is a gift of God."*

Philippians 4: *"Rejoice in the Lord always and again I say, Rejoice."*

James 4: *"Submit yourselves therefore to God, resist the Devil, and he will flee from you."*

1 John 4: *"Beloved, if God so loved us, we ought also to love one another."*

Acknowledgements

Anyone that spends any time with me knows that I have a deep passion to share the Gospel with anyone who will listen. God has burdened my heart with this great desire. The problem is that I am easily distracted, a bit lazy, and extremely unorganized. Why God called me of all people to write a book like this is...well just like God. God often calls us to do things that are totally out of our comfort zone! The amazing part is that God has truly been with me all the way. The Holy Spirit has led me through every step of this Amazing experience. So, I want to first acknowledge my Lord and Savior Jesus Christ who has radically changed my life and has given me a passion to help others find their purpose in Christ.

The first person I would like to thank is my beautiful wife Emily who has allowed me the time needed to work on this book. As long as it took me to finish it I'm not certain that she believed I was even working on it. (There were occasional instances where I could have dozed off, or watched a little football). In any case, if not for her support and prayers I would have never finished this book, so thank you so much Emily. God certainly led me to you and I'm forever grateful for your friendship.

I would also like to thank my 4 children Logan, Jonathan, Nathan, and Kathryn. Of course, they probably have no idea that I was even writing a book. Logan was on his phone, Jonathan and Nathan were playing their PlayStation, and Kathryn was simply being Kathryn. Thanks Kids, you are wonderful gifts of God who give my life such Joy and I'm proud of all of you...yes, you too Logan.

I need to thank my Mom for all the prayers she has prayed on my behalf. I needed every one of them. You are probably the most surprised that I would even graduate High School much less write a book. Thanks for putting up with all my antics over the years. You can attest to the power of prayer.

To those of you whom have sat through any Bible Study or Sunday School Class that I have taught, you will never get that time back...sorry. You have truly blessed me, especially the Senior Saints Sunday School Class. I have indeed learned more from you than I have ever taught any of you. Thank you for allowing me to share the Gospel as well as my heart with you guys.

I have been blessed to have served under some of the Godliest Pastors and teachers, I cannot tell you enough how much you all have meant to me. First, I want to thank Lee Delbridge who baptized me at Northside Christian Church in Columbus Ga, when I was 11 years old. Yes, I remember, and I still have the hot wheel you gave me. Tony Sullivan who not only officiated my wedding at Maranatha Christian Church but taught me you can have fun and be a Christian. Carl Beckham and Don Boswell who pastored my years at Cross Plains Christian Church. Doug New who I have the utmost respect for and encouraged me to finish this book. Shane Roberson who is one of the most anointed men I have ever met. Joel Sutherland who also encouraged me to write this book. Hal Waters, my current pastor at Midway West.

To anyone associated with Faith Bible Institute I could not thank any of you enough. Even though I have never met him, John Yates inspired me to write this book and most of what is in this book was taught to me by John. John instructs Faith Bible

Institute, which is a 3 year in depth study of the Bible. God used this class to inspire me to write this book. I would highly recommend taking Faith Bible Institute. A large reason for writing this book is to lead more Christians to spend more time in God's Word. There is no better way to dive into the deep truths of God's Word than to enroll in John Yates Faith Bible Institute.

I would also like to thank one of my dearest friends, Howard Brooks who has allowed me to join him in the prison ministry as well as ministering to the elderly. He has been such a blessing to me and my family, thank you so much Brother Howard.

I am not a gifted writer. I can write 5 pages without using the first period. Special thanks go to Debbie Williams who spent many hours editing this book so that maybe you could understand it...Thanks so much Debbie.

To every one of my co-workers at the TMC, I would like to thank you guys for putting up with me for so long. You guys can certainly attest to the fact that if God can use someone as messed up as me then God can help ANYBODY!

Of all the people who have supported and blessed me there are 3 very special men that God has placed in my life. These men have helped me to become the person I am today. They taught me how to live the Christian life, and I can't thank them enough. The first is my Father-in-Law Billy Horton who was one of the hardest working men I ever met. He was a big man in every way. He intimidated me as he was Emily's dad and there are times I believe he wanted to strangle me. Thankfully, the only thing bigger than his body was his heart. He truly loved others. He loved to work and he could build or fix anything. He used his ability to help in numerous projects at the church. Not only did

Billy work on many Church building projects, He would help anyone who asked for help. He truly used his talent to help others and while I can't hammer a nail to save my life, Billy inspires me to use my ability to help others as well. Billy passed away but his character and his heart lives on. Thanks Billy, for teaching me the value of a good work ethic and of the importance of using your abilities to help others.

Growing up I only saw my dad on the weekends as he worked many long hours at UPS. When he was not working he spent his time with his family or at Church. He taught me the importance of not only going to church but serving Christ within the church. He would lead singing every Sunday morning, he served as Deacon and if the church doors were open he would be there ready to serve. I may be a little biased, but he was one of the kindest men I have ever met.

I remember when Logan was a little toddler dad would love spending time with him. He would take him to work, to the park, and of course to church. I remember when he retired I'm sure he was looking forward to tinkering on stuff. God had other ideas as Emily and I had twins Jonathan and Nathan. We needed help with childcare for twins, so he kept them while we went to work. He loved my boys so much. He was a great dad, but he was the best grand dad! I often wonder how things would be if dad had not passed away. I know God is in control and that He loves us, but when my dad passed away I had a hard time. Through those dark days that followed Jesus never left me, his presence gave me the peace I needed to get through. Although I miss my dad, I am so thankful to have been blessed with such a Godly dad. I am certain if there are any back roads in Heaven that Dad knows them all well.

Finally, I would like to thank one of the most amazing men on earth, my Grandaddy Paschal. He is my hero in many ways. He is a part of what Tom Brokaw calls the greatest generation. He joined the Army Air Force as World War 2 began. He was the radio operator on a B-25 bomber in the Pacific. He doesn't talk too much about the time he spent there, but he lets anyone who asks know that God's hand was on him and on all who served and continue to serve in the military. He is not unlike any other WWII veteran I have met. They truly are a special generation of people whom we all could learn from.

Beyond being a WWII vet Grandaddy is one of the best listeners I have ever met. One of my favorite places on Earth is swinging under Grandaddy's pecan tree. I have spent many hours under that pecan tree talking to Grandaddy while he patiently listens to all my stories. When I told him about writing this book he wanted to know if he could help in any way. I couldn't think of anything, so he just handed me a check and told me to use the money to help with getting the book published. It's been nearly 2 years since he wrote that check and every time we talk he asks how the book is coming? Well, thanks to you, I finally could finish the book and I hope you enjoy it. Thanks for all that you have done for me.

Notes

All scripture used throughout book are from The King James Version.

The cover's image is from

https://unityinthetruth.files.wordpress.com/2012/10/bible-light-bulb-image.jpgm

Introduction.

1. transcripts.cnn.com/TRANSCRIPTS/0512/02/lkl.01.html Larry King Live Dec 2nd 2005

2. Strobel, Lee. *The case for the real Jesus: a journalist investigates current attacks on the identity of Christ.* Grand Rapids, MI: Zondervan/ Willow Creek Resources, 2014. Pg 233.

3. Strobel, Lee. *The case for the real Jesus: a journalist investigates current attacks on the identity of Christ.* Grand Rapids, MI: Zondervan/ Willow Creek Resources, 2014. Pg 246-249

4. Geisler, Norman L. ; Turek, Frank. *I Don't Have Enough Faith to be an Athiest.* Wheaton, Il: Crossway, 2004. Pg. 66-69.

The Bible is historically true.

1. Wilmington, Harold L. *Willmington's Guide to the Bible 30th Anniversary Edition.* Tyndale House Publishers, 2011. pg.661-662

2. Strobel, Lee. *The case for the real Jesus: a journalist investigates current attacks on the identity of Christ.* Grand Rapids, MI: Zondervan/ Willow Creek Resources, 2014. pg 82-85

3. Geisler, Norman L. ; Turek, Frank. *I Don't Have Enough Faith to be an Athiest.* Wheaton, Il: Crossway, 2004. pg225

4. Geisler, Norman L. ; Turek, Frank. *I Don't Have Enough Faith to be an Athiest.* Wheaton, Il: Crossway, 2004. Pg. 230

5. Feiler, Bruce. *Walking The Bible A journey by Land through the five books of Moses.* New York, NY: Harper Collins Publishers, 2001 pg 211-213

6. Geisler, Norman L. ; Turek, Frank. *I Don't Have Enough Faith to be an Athiest.* Wheaton, Il: Crossway, 2004 pg. 368-370

7. Strobel, Lee. *The case for the real Jesus: a journalist investigates current attacks on the identity of Christ.* Grand Rapids, MI: Zondervan/ Willow Creek Resources, 2014. Pg.70-71

8. Wilmington, Harold L. *Willmington's Guide to the Bible 30th Anniversary Edition.* Tyndale House Publishers, 2011. Pg. 687-688

9. Strobel, Lee. *The case for the real Jesus: a journalist investigates current attacks on the identity of Christ.*

Grand Rapids, MI: Zondervan/ Willow Creek Resources, 2014. Pg 85-86

10. Wilmington, Harold L. *Willmington's Guide to the Bible 30th Anniversary Edition.* Tyndale House Publishers, 2011. Pg. 689

11. Geisler, Norman L. ; Turek, Frank. *I Don't Have Enough Faith to be an Athiest.* Wheaton, Il: Crossway, 2004 pg 371-372

12. Feiler, Bruce. *Walking The Bible A journey by Land through the five books of Moses.* New York, NY: Harper Collins Publishers, 2001 pg. 105-107

13. McDowell, Josh. *The New Evidence that demands a verdict.* Nashville, TN: Thomas Nelson Publishers, 1999 pg. 61-65

14. Wilmington, Harold L. *Willmington's Guide to the Bible 30th Anniversary Edition.* Tyndale House Publishers, 2011. Pg 684-687

15. Feiler, Bruce. *Walking The Bible A journey by Land through the five books of Moses.* New York, NY: Harper Collins Publishers, 2001 Quotes from Fieler are found on Pg 243, 408, & 409.

16. McDowell, Josh. *The New Evidence that demands a verdict.* Nashville, TN: Thomas Nelson Publishers, 1999 pg. 54-57

17. Marano, Paul ; O'Rielly, Bill. *Killing Jesus.* Baltimore: Winkler Media, 2013.

18. Wilmington, Harold L. *Willmington's Guide to the Bible 30th Anniversary Edition.* Tyndale House Publishers, 2011. Pg. 484-485

19. Marano, Paul ; O'Rielly, Bill. *Killing Jesus.* Baltimore: Winkler Media, 2013

20. Wilmington, Harold L. *Willmington's Guide to the Bible 30th Anniversary Edition.* Tyndale House Publishers, 2011. Pg 514-515

The Bible is Scientifically reliable.

1. www.merton.ox.ac.uk/sites/merton.ox.ac.uk/files/attachments/Chapel-Services-Trinity2014.pdf

2. https://christianheritagefellowship.com/the-christian-founding-of-harvard/

3. http://www.ptsem.edu/about/history

4. Buckley, William F. *God and man at Yale: the superstitions of "academic freedom".* Washington, D.C.: Gateway Editions, 2002.

5. http://www.icr.org/article/newton/

6. http://www.christianity.com/church/church-history/timeline/1601-1700/robert-boyle-father-of-modern-chemistry-11630103.html

7. https://www.thegospelcoalition.org/article/pascals-method-for-presenting-the-christian-faith

8. http://creation.com/johannes-kepler

9. http://www.godandscience.org/apologetics/sciencefait h.html

10. http://www.reasons.org/blogs/reflections/christian-thinkers-101-a-crash-course-on-blaise-pascal

11. http://creationsciencehalloffame.org/inductees/deceas ed/joseph-lister/

12. https://www.faraday.st-edmunds.cam.ac.uk/Faraday.php

13. http://www.christianitytoday.com/ct/2002/novemberw eb-only/11-4-21.0.html

14. http://news.nationalgeographic.com/2015/03/150319-three-questions-francis-collins-nih-science/

15. http://www.popsci.com/article/science/meet-scientist-who-might-end-climate-culture-wars

16. Morris, Henry M. *The Biblical Basis for Modern Science* Green Forest, AR: Master Books New Leaf Publishing, 2010. Pg 88-89.

17. https://answersingenesis.org/creation-scientists/

18. Sarfati, Jonathan. *Refuting Evolution* Green Forest, AR: Master Books New Leaf Publishing, 2003. Quote on page 29.

19. Geisler, Norman L. ; Turek, Frank. *I Don't Have Enough Faith to be an Athiest.* Wheaton, Il: Crossway, 2004. Pg 118

20. Hawking, Stephen. *A brief history of time: from the big bang to black holes.* London: Bantam Books, 2016.

21. Walt, Brown. *In the Beginning; Compelling evidence for creation and the flood* Walt Brown 2001. Pg 69

22. http://www.physicsoftheuniverse.com/scientists_lemai tre.html

23. Sarfati, Jonathan. *Refuting Evolution* Green Forest, AR: Master Books New Leaf Publishing, 2003. Quote on page 92-93.

24. Walt, Brown. *In the Beginning; Compelling evidence for creation and the flood* Walt Brown 2001. Pg. 25

25. Morris, Henry M. *The Biblical Basis for Modern Science* Green Forest, AR: Master Books New Leaf Publishing, 2010. Pg. 132-133.

26. https://www.livescience.com/2896-oldest-rocks-earth.html https://map.gsfc.nasa.gov/

27. In the Beginning Pg.31-34. Walt, Brown. *In the Beginning; Compelling evidence for creation and the flood* Walt Brown 2001. Pg. 31-33

28. Morris, Henry M. *The Biblical Basis for Modern Science* Green Forest, AR: Master Books New Leaf Publishing, 2010.

29. Walt, Brown. *In the Beginning; Compelling evidence for creation and the flood* Walt Brown 2001

30. http://www.icr.org/article/dating-niagara-falls/

31. Morris, Henry M. *The Biblical Basis for Modern Science* Green Forest, AR: Master Books New Leaf Publishing, 2010.

32. Geisler, Norman L. ; Turek, Frank. *I Don't Have Enough Faith to be an Athiest.* Wheaton, Il: Crossway, 2004.

33. Morris, Henry M. *The Biblical Basis for Modern Science* Green Forest, AR: Master Books New Leaf Publishing, 2010.

34. Sarfati, Jonathan. *Refuting Evolution* Green Forest, AR: Master Books New Leaf Publishing, 2003.

35. Morris, Henry M. *The Biblical Basis for Modern Science* Green Forest, AR: Master Books New Leaf Publishing, 2010.

36. Sarfati, Jonathan. *Refuting Evolution* Green Forest, AR: Master Books New Leaf Publishing, 2003. This quote is on Pg 51.

37. Morris, Henry M. *The Biblical Basis for Modern Science* Green Forest, AR: Master Books New Leaf Publishing, 2010.

38. Sarfati, Jonathan. *Refuting Evolution* Green Forest, AR: Master Books New Leaf Publishing, 2003. Pg. 82-83.

39. Morris, Henry M. *The Biblical Basis for Modern Science* Green Forest, AR: Master Books New Leaf Publishing, 2010. Pg. 201-203.

40. http://www.icr.org/article/anti-evolutionary-secrets-bonobo-genome/

41. Sarfati, Jonathan. *Refuting Evolution* Green Forest, AR: Master Books New Leaf Publishing, 2003. Pg. 22, 91.

42. Geisler, Norman L. ; Turek, Frank. *I Don't Have Enough Faith to be an Athiest.* Wheaton, Il: Crossway, 2004. Pg. 176-179.

43. Morris, Henry M. *The Biblical Basis for Modern Science* Green Forest, AR: Master Books New Leaf Publishing, 2010.

44. Walt, Brown. *In the Beginning; Compelling evidence for creation and the flood* Walt Brown 2001.

45. Morris, Henry M. *The Biblical Basis for Modern Science* Green Forest, AR: Master Books New Leaf Publishing, 2010.

46. Walt, Brown. *In the Beginning; Compelling evidence for creation and the flood* Walt Brown 2001. Pg. 249-250.

47. Morris, Henry M. *The Biblical Basis for Modern Science* Green Forest, AR: Master Books New Leaf Publishing, 2010.

48. Geisler, Norman L. ; Turek, Frank. *I Don't Have Enough Faith to be an Athiest.* Wheaton, Il: Crossway, 2004. Pg. 350-353.

49. Morris, Henry M. *The Biblical Basis for Modern Science* Green Forest, AR: Master Books New Leaf Publishing, 2010. Pg. 57-58.

The Bible is Prophetically Accurate

1. Stoner, Peter Winebrenner., and Robert C. Newman. *Science speaks: scientific proof of the accuracy of prophecy and the Bible*. Chicago: Moody Press, 1976. Chapter 2.

2. *Nelsons concordance to the Bible: dictionary of proper names and subject index* London: Thomas Nelson and Sons. Pg 897-898.

3. Wilmington, Harold L. *Willmington's Guide to the Bible 30th Anniversary Edition*. Tyndale House Publishers, 2011. Pg. 155.

4. *Nelsons concordance to the Bible: dictionary of proper names and subject index* London: Thomas Nelson and Sons. Pg. 1282-1283.

5. Yates, John T. *Faith Bible Institute Volume 1* Monroe, LA Faith Bible Institute Press, 2013. Pg. 253-254.

6. *Nelsons concordance to the Bible: dictionary of proper names and subject index* London: Thomas Nelson and Sons. Pg. 148-149.

7. Yates, John T. *Faith Bible Institute Volume 1* Monroe, LA Faith Bible Institute Press, 2013. Pg 252-253

8. *Nelsons concordance to the Bible: dictionary of proper names and subject index* London: Thomas Nelson and Sons. Pg 1116-1117.

9. Geisler, Norman L. ; Turek, Frank. *I Don't Have Enough Faith to be an Athiest.* Wheaton, II: Crossway, 2004. Pg. 341-343.

10. Wilmington, Harold L. *Willmington's Guide to the Bible 30th Anniversary Edition.* Tyndale House Publishers, 2011. Pg. 178-182.

11. http://christinprophecy.org/articles/the-gate-to-prophecy

12. Ithttp://www.watchmanbiblestudy.com/Articles/1948ProoheciesFulfilled.html

13. McDowell, Josh. *The New Evidence that demands a verdict.* Nashville, TN: Thomas Nelson Publishers, 1999

14. Tenth Avenue North. *Worn, The Struggle.* 2012. https://www.youtube.com/watch?v=UUEy8nZvpdM

15. Wilmington, Harold L. *Willmington's Guide to the Bible 30th Anniversary Edition.* Tyndale House Publishers, 2011.

16. Lowry, Robert. *Nothing but the Blood* The United Methodist Hymnal, NO 362.

17. Geisler, Norman L. ; Turek, Frank. *I Don't Have Enough Faith to be an Athiest.* Wheaton, Il: Crossway, 2004 pg. 329-338.

18. http://www.thenazareneway.com/details_history_of_cr ucifixion.htm

19. http://catholicinsight.com/the-physical-effects-of-the-scourging-and-crucifixion-of-jesus/

20. McGee, John Vernon. *Thru the Bible Commentary Series PSALMS 1-41* Nashville, TN: Thomas Nelson Publishers, 1991. Pg. 121-132.

21. Yates, John T. *Faith Bible Institute Volume 6* Monroe, LA Faith Bible Institute Press, 2013. Pg. 652 Revelation outline.

22. Hill, Jim. *What a Day that will be* 1955. https://www.youtube.com/watch?v=0W1zT4SE_go

23. Yates, John T. *Faith Bible Institute Volume 6* Monroe, LA Faith Bible Institute Press, 2013 pg. 669-671.

24. Wilmington, Harold L. *Willmington's Guide to the Bible 30th Anniversary Edition.* Tyndale House Publishers, 2011. Pg. 313-314.

25. Yates, John T. *Faith Bible Institute Volume 6* Monroe, LA Faith Bible Institute Press, 2013. Pg. 352-355.

The Bible is Spiritually Sound

1. Yates, John T. *Faith Bible Institute Volume 4* Monroe, LA Faith Bible Institute Press, 2013. This entire chapter is

heavily influenced by John Yates teachings on the doctrine of salvation.

2. Wilmington, Harold L. *Willmington's Guide to the Bible 30th Anniversary Edition*. Tyndale House Publishers, 2011. Pg. 540-541.

3. West, Matthew." *Hello My Name is" Into The Light* 2012.

https://www.youtube.com/watch?v=ZuJWQzjfU3o

4. Wilkinson, Bruce. *Secrets of the Vine; Breaking through to Abundance* Sisters, OR: Multnomah Publishers 2001. Pg.17-27.

5. Geisler, Norman L. ; Turek, Frank. *I Don't Have Enough Faith to be an Athiest*. Wheaton, Il: Crossway, 2004

6. Wilmington, Harold L. *Willmington's Guide to the Bible 30th Anniversary Edition*. Tyndale House Publishers, 2011 Quotes from pg. 554-555.

7. Spafford, Horatio, *It is Well with my Soul* 1873. https://www.youtube.com/watch?v=T8_EfDqF7Y

8. Keller, Timothy, *The Reason for God; Belief in an age of Skepticism* New York, NY: Riverhead Books 2008. Quote is found on Pg. 202

9. Wilmington, Harold L. *Willmington's Guide to the Bible 30th Anniversary Edition*. Tyndale House Publishers, 2011 pg 503.

10. Big Daddy Weave *"Redeemed" Love Come to Life* 2012. https://www.youtube.com/watch?v=VzGAYNKDyIU

11. Wilmington, Harold L. *Willmington's Guide to the Bible 30th Anniversary Edition*. Tyndale House Publishers, 2011 Quote found on pg. 509-510.

12. Keller, Timothy, *The Reason for God; Belief in an age of Skepticism* New York, NY: Riverhead Books 2008. Quote is found on pg. 210.

13. www.britannica.com/list/10-failed-doomsday-predictions

14. http://www.watchmanbiblestudy.com/Articles/1948PropheciesFulfilled.html

15. Yates, John T. *Faith Bible Institute Volume 4* Monroe, LA Faith Bible Institute Press, 2013. Pg 507-508

16. Bethke, Jefferson, *Jesus > Religion: Why He Is So Much Better Than Trying Harder, Doing More, and ...* Thomas Nelson Publishers 2013. Pg. 150-151.

17. Wilkinson, Bruce. *Secrets of the Vine; Breaking through to Abundance* Sisters, OR: Multnomah Publishers 2001.

Taking God at His Word

You can contact me at godathisword@gmail.com

For updates on events go to
godathisword.wix.com/website

Made in the USA
Columbia, SC
29 April 2022